HAVE I GOT NEWS FOR YOU

FOR YOU

THE QUIZ OF 2022

WRITTEN BY DAN BOWMAN

SPHERE

SPHERE

First published in Great Britain in 2022 by Sphere

1 3 5 7 9 10 8 6 4 2

Copyright © Hat Trick Productions Ltd 2022
Written by Dan Bowman

A CIP catalogue record for this book
is available from the British Library.

ISBN 978-1-4087-2710-2

Typeset in Plantin by M Rules
Printed and bound in Great Britain by Clays Ltd, Elcograf S.p.A.

Papers used by Sphere are from well-managed forests
and other responsible sources.

MIX
Paper from
responsible sources
FSC® C104740

Sphere
An imprint of
Little, Brown Book Group
Carmelite House
50 Victoria Embankment
London EC4Y 0DZ

An Hachette UK Company
www.hachette.co.uk

www.littlebrown.co.uk

INTRODUCTION

Hello, and welcome to *Have I Got News for You: The Quiz of 2022*.*

What a year it's been. If Billy Joel had tried to write 'We Didn't Start the Fire' about 2022 he'd have run out of space and given up after seeing the price of paper. Russia invaded Ukraine, Boris Johnson resigned, the Queen passed the baton to Charles after a seventy-year reign, heat records were broken, food and energy bills went through the roof, trains didn't run, planes didn't take off, fading celebrities discovered that libel laws are a great way to generate publicity, Keir Starmer furrowed his brow slightly harder than usual, Liz Truss spent more money in her first week as PM than anyone since the war, and – as usual – most of the biggest stories broke while *Have I Got News for You* was off the air.

What better way, then, to commemorate a year most of us probably want to forget than with lots and lots (and lots) of quiz questions about it? There's the Missing Words Round, the Odd One Out Round, loads of rounds that we've nicked from other puzzle books, and for any insomniacs out there, there's even one on the Labour Party.

So, sit back, relax, light a candle (or if you're doing really well, a paraffin lamp) and see how much you can remember from one of the most chaotic years in modern history.

---

* *This book went to print in September 2022. We can't see into the future (and indeed, Prime Minister Liz says we shouldn't even try), which is why there aren't any questions on the last few months of the year, and why there might be occasional mentions of some people who've selfishly died in the meantime.*

New Year, Same Old Rubbish

As we left 2021, there were rumblings of illicit soirées at Downing Street and Russia appeared to be mobilising troops along the Ukrainian border, but we'd come through Christmas without another lockdown so there were high hopes for a stable, prosperous year. Hang on – sorry – wrong notes, that was 2012. Let's see if you can answer these questions from the start of 2022 instead.

1. Which band performed on the BBC's reliably dreadful New Year's Eve show, managing to see in 2022 and outrage the eternally outraged in the process?

    A. Years and Years
    B. Bastille
    C. Blossoms
    D. Bring Me the Horizon

2. NFTs set the tone for another terrible year by becoming the must-have investment for the worst people you know, but what does NFT stand for?

    A. Numbered Financial Token
    B. Non-financial Transaction
    C. Non-fungible Token
    D. Negative Forecast Trend

3. The Tories easily won the Southend West by-election at the beginning of February, but which party came second?

    A. The Liberal Democrats

    B. UKIP

    C. Reform UK

    D. The Psychedelic Movement

4. In the first of many potentially apocalyptic events of 2022, scientists discovered that one of Elon Musk's old rockets was on course to hit what at 5,700mph?

    A. The moon

    B. Antarctica

    C. The International Space Station

    D. Mars

5. The UK Singles Chart was topped by an original song from a Disney film for the first time ever, but what was it called?

    A. We Don't Talk About Bruno

    B. I Refuse to Discuss Barbara

    C. Please, Nobody Mention Rupert

    D. Restraining Order Against Grandad

6. During the launch of the government's 'Levelling Up' scheme, Michael Gove said he had what for Dominic Cummings?

    A. No respect whatsoever
    B. A deep reservoir of affection
    C. Unparalleled, endless resentment
    D. Vast reserves of admiration

7. Word-guessing game Wordle became a viral sensation in early 2022, but who was it originally created for?

    A. Sixth-form college students
    B. Children off school with Covid
    C. The creator's wife
    D. The creator's children

8. Which UK reality show announced plans for a spin-off stage musical?

    A. *Love Island*
    B. *The Apprentice*
    C. *Come Dine With Me*
    D. *The Great British Bake Off*

9. Which YouTuber was revealed as the platform's top earner in 2021?

    A. PewDiePie
    B. Zoella
    C. MrBeast
    D. Steve Terreberry

10. In a desperate attempt to remain relevant (until 2024 at least . . .) Donald Trump launched his new social media platform in February. What is it called?

   A. Truth Social
   B. Patriot Book
   C. MAGA Central
   D. Scorn Hub

NEW YEAR, SAME OLD RUBBISH – ANSWERS

1. A – Years and Years's performance received 179 complaints for being 'overly sexualised' by people seemingly unaware that midnight occurs after the watershed.

2. C – NFTs, or 'non-fungible tokens' gave people the impossible choice between buying a new house or a JPEG of a monkey wearing a Stetson. And you get an extra point for knowing what 'fungible' means.

3. D – None of the major opposition parties contested the election out of respect to former MP Sir David Amess, who was tragically murdered in October 2021. UKIP did, however, and amassed a whopping four hundred votes to finish third behind political heavyweights The Psychedelic Movement.

4. A – No dystopian nightmare would be complete without an appearance from Elon Musk, who thankfully stopped short of calling the moon a paedophile.

5. A – Taken from the *Encanto* soundtrack and buoyed by TikTok parodies, 'We Don't Talk About Bruno' provided joy for children and PTSD for parents.

6. B – Gove made the comments in spite of Cummings's repeated berating of the government. He declined to go into more detail about his 'deep reservoir' however, coming as welcome news to people who were eating at the time.

7. C – Creator Josh Wardle (which is where Wordle's name comes from) came up with the idea in 2013 and spent the following years perfecting it on the basis that his wife enjoys puzzles, although it'd probably have been simpler to pop down to the shops for a crossword book.

8. D – Plans for a musical version of the long-running baking show were of huge interest to anyone wondering how Matt Lucas and Noel Fielding's obvious lack of enthusiasm could be captured in song.

9. C – Jimmy Donaldson – better known as MrBeast – made an eye-watering $54 million after becoming the world's leading authority in the lucrative 'owning a webcam and reacting to things' industry.

10. A – The launch of Truth Social was mired in technical issues and criticism of its terms of service, but was a godsend for people who enjoy being screamed at by an elderly man while he uses the toilet. Despite banning Trump's account, Twitter ensured it remained a world leader in misinformation by allowing official Russian ones to stay up.

Record Breakers

Although 'fixed penalty notices received by a single government' wasn't officially recognised as a world record this year, plenty of things were. Here are ten questions about all things biggest, longest and oldest in 2022.

1. Early in the year, the bizarrely named TobyKeith was confirmed as the world's oldest what?

    A. Cat
    B. Tortoise
    C. Fish
    D. Dog

2. In another age record, a French woman became the world's oldest living person in April when the previous holder died in Japan. What other record does she hold?

    A. Oldest European of all time
    B. Most popes met
    C. Oldest Covid-19 survivor
    D. Most boiled eggs eaten in sixty seconds

3. Welsh farmer Gerwyn Jones sold what for a record-breaking £189,000?

    A. Bull

    B. Sheepdog

    C. Racing pigeon

    D. Tractor

4. In May, 1,369 people descended on the town of Whitby in Yorkshire to break the record for the most people dressed as which fictional character?

    A. Spider-Man

    B. Frankenstein's monster

    C. Count Dracula

    D. Darth Vader

5. A painting by which artist became the most expensive piece of twentieth-century art ever after selling at auction in 2022?

    A. Andy Warhol

    B. Pablo Picasso

    C. Paul Cézanne

    D. Frida Kahlo

6. A hundred-year-old Brazilian man broke the record for the longest time doing what?

   A. Owning the same house
   B. Living in a tree
   C. Holding a driving licence
   D. Working for the same company

7. While much of the UK was enjoying the jubilee festivities on 2 June, four hundred Brits gathered at Plymouth lido dressed as what?

   A. Scuba divers
   B. Mermaids
   C. Pirates
   D. Aliens

8. As part of National Vegetarian Week, a chef from Wiltshire set a new world record after creating the largest-ever what?

   A. Omelette
   B. Pizza
   C. Ball of falafel
   D. Scotch egg

9. Daniel Alcon, a thirty-five-year-old schoolteacher from Wimbledon, set a new world record in 2022 by doing what for almost forty hours?

    A. Teaching maths
    B. Freestyle rapping
    C. Sitting in a bath of beans
    D. Running laps of a playground

10. When Anoushe Husain climbed 1,229 feet and 9 inches at The Castle Climbing Centre in London, what made the feat especially impressive?

    A. She did it blindfolded
    B. She was only six years old
    C. She completed it in one hour
    D. She did it one-handed

Record Breakers – Answers

1. D – Chihuahua TobyKeith (named after US singer ... well, Toby Keith) broke the record for oldest living dog on 16 March at twenty-one years and sixty-six days, and – as is the custom when you're ancient – put his long life down to twenty cigarettes a day and a glass of sherry before bed.

2. C – Sister André (born Lucile Randon in 1904) became the world's oldest Covid survivor when she recovered from the virus in 2021. Then, at the age of 118 years and seventy-three days she became the world's oldest living person when 119-year-old Kane Tanaka died on 19 April. The curse of being the world's oldest person strikes yet again; someone should really look into why they keep dying.

3. A – The Limousin bull – named Graiggoch Rambo – broke the record for its breed after selling for six figures at auction. Rambo's new owner says aside from stopping off at a china shop on the way home he has no regrets over the purchase.

4. C – Bram Stoker got the idea for *Dracula* while visiting Whitby, after he heard a bloke in the pub say, 'hey, someone should write a book about a vampire'.

5. A – Andy Warhol's famous image of Marilyn Monroe sold for an eye-watering $195 million, or $195,000,005 with postage.

6. D – Walter Orthman, who turned one hundred in April, has worked at the same textiles company in Brazil since 1938 and often comes out on top in office disputes simply by outliving his colleagues.

7. B – The gathering was officially confirmed to have the most people dressed as mermaids in one place at the same time. Good job they got the record really or they'd have been going home with their tails between their legs.

8. D – The egg at the centre of the, erm, Scotch was of the ostrich variety, which took chef Leigh Evans more than ninety minutes to boil. Must be doing well for himself if he can afford to boil an egg in 2022.

9. B – School teacher Alcon, who raps under an alias of DAlcon, broke the previous freestyle rapping record of thirty-six hours. The Guinness World Records judge who witnessed the attempt congratulated Mr Alcon for the feat but begged him never to do it again as it was the most boring two days of his life.

10. D – Husain, originally from Luxembourg and co-founder of the Paraclimbing London group, was born with her right forearm missing, and broke the world record for 'greatest vertical distance climbed on a climbing wall with one hand in one hour'. If that wasn't mind-boggling enough, she completed the feat using the weaker side of her body.

SUNLIT UPLANDS OR: HOW I LEARNED TO STOP WORRYING AND LOVE BREXIT

If there's one thing we can all agree on, it's whether or not leaving the EU was a good idea. Fortunately (for the purposes of this book at least) Brexit is very much still in the news, so see if you can take back control of these ten questions.

1. After spending a few years wandering along the south coast and angrily pointing at the sea, Nigel Farage returned from political limbo and suggested another referendum on what?

    A. Abolishing the House of Lords
    B. Net zero targets
    C. Withdrawing from NATO
    D. Re-joining the EU

2. As part of a mini reshuffle in early February as No. 10 tried to move on from partygate, Jacob Rees-Mogg was named Minister for ...

    A. European Relations
    B. Taking Back Control
    C. Global Britain
    D. Brexit Opportunities

3. Boris Johnson caused outrage at the Conservative Party's spring conference when he compared the EU referendum to what?

   A. The Normandy landings
   B. *Sophie's Choice*
   C. The war in Ukraine
   D. The persecution of Jesus

4. Early in 2022 the Public Accounts Committee predicted Brexit free-trade arrangements could deliver how many economic benefits?

   A. None
   B. 1–3
   C. 4–5
   D. More than 10

5. During his spring budget statement, Rishi Sunak claimed that thanks to Brexit he was able to axe VAT on what?

   A. Champagne
   B. Solar panels
   C. Concrete
   D. Gold bullion

6. In one of 2022's more peculiar Brexit headlines, it was alleged that new trade laws had 'squashed' which UK industry?

    A. Highlighter pens

    B. Lip fillers

    C. Edible insects

    D. Vibrators

7. The so-called 'Festival of Brexit' finally got underway, with the first event taking place at Caernarfon Castle in Wales, but what is the festival's official title?

    A. National Festival of Creativity

    B. Unboxed

    C. Resurgence

    D. Glastonbollocks

8. As part of the festival's 'celebrations', it was announced what would be installed in Weston-super-Mare?

    A. A fibreglass T-Rex

    B. A sixty-foot metal scorpion

    C. A replica of the *Titanic*

    D. A decommissioned oil rig

9. Which of the following politicians doesn't have 'Brexit Secretary' on their CV?

    A. David Frost

    B. Dominic Raab

    C. David Davis

    D. Steve Barclay

10. Which musical opted to tour the EU with a Chinese production, claiming Brexit 'red tape' made it too expensive to use a British one?

    A. *Charlie and the Chocolate Factory*

    B. *Wicked*

    C. *The Phantom of the Opera*

    D. *The Book of Mormon*

Sunlit Uplands or: How I Learned to Stop Worrying and Love Brexit – Answers

1. B – It was the government's net zero targets that old Nige' decided to take exception to, saying, 'It's a little bit like the European question. Everybody agrees and you're not allowed to have your say', referring to the thing nobody can agree on that we had a referendum for.

2. D – As well as seeking out Brexit opportunities (which consisted solely of pleading with *Sun* readers to help him find them) Rees-Mogg was also tasked with overseeing government efficiency, as the current model of accepting shady donations is painfully slow.

3. C – Incredibly, Boris Johnson managed to compare people voting for Brexit to Ukrainians fighting off the Russian invasion, causing a mini-stampede in the process as Nadine Dorries and Michael Fabricant raced to anyone with a microphone to blindly defend him.

4. A – The committee predicted that we could potentially see no benefits whatsoever, although it's unclear how they reached that conclusion when we're famously getting that £350 million-a-week boost to the economy.

5. B – The installation of solar panels is marginally cheaper thanks to Brexit apparently. Must be all those extra rays from the sunlit uplands.

6. C – As companies that produce edible insects furiously urged the government to rectify the situation, No. 10

admitted there were a few bugs in the system but warned not to make a meal of it.

7. B – The kick-off event for Unboxed involved projecting images onto Caernarfon Castle and included mammoth attractions such as 'local choir' and 'some drawings from a nearby school'.

8. D – The attraction, called 'See Monster', will see a decommissioned oil rig dumped into the town's former lido, and is expected to boost Weston-super-Mare's tourism by up to twelve people.

9. A – Only Raab, Davis and Barclay were Brexit secretaries. David Frost did however work on the Brexit deal, being chief negotiator and the PM's Europe advisor before spectacularly resigning over terms that he'd negotiated himself.

10. C – It was *The Phantom of the Opera* that was hit by red tape. Brexiteers reacted furiously to the news, presumably as the tape was red and not blue.

WHERE IN THE WORLD . . .

The answers to the following questions are geographical – which, unless you're Dominic Raab, shouldn't prove too difficult.

1. The roof of which UK landmark was severely damaged by Storm Eunice in February?

    A. The Eden Project
    B. Brighton Pavilion
    C. The O2 Arena
    D. Shakespeare's Globe

2. Which seaside town hosted the Conservative Party's 2022 spring conference?

    A. Bournemouth
    B. Margate
    C. Blackpool
    D. Skegness

3. Where was current US President Joe Biden born?

    A. Pennsylvania
    B. Wyoming
    C. South Dakota
    D. The Garden of Eden

4. Which African country did the Home Office unveil plans to relocate asylum seekers to?

   A. Rwanda

   B. Zambia

   C. Malawi

   D. Somalia

5. Going a bit further afield, in early 2022 scientists discovered unexpected and dramatic changes in the temperature of which planet?

   A. Mercury

   B. Neptune

   C. Uranus

   D. Saturn

6. In 2022 Radio One DJ Jordan North raised over £500,000 for Comic Relief by sailing from London to which northern town?

   A. Blackburn

   B. Rochdale

   C. Huddersfield

   D. Burnley

7. Early in the year Adele was forced to cancel a twenty-four-show residency in which city?

   A. London

   B. Las Vegas

   C. Zürich

   D. Johannesburg

8. In 2022 ITV dramatised the infamous story of 'canoe man' John Darwin. Which British seaside resort did he paddle out from when he faked his death?

   A. Barton-on-Sea
   B. Skegness
   C. Seaton Carew
   D. Milford Haven

9. After two years of being held virtually, Radio One's Big Weekend resumed as an in-person event in 2022, being held in which city?

   A. Dundee
   B. Ipswich
   C. Hereford
   D. Coventry

10. Amazon was reported to be planning 260 supermarkets in the UK over the next three years, but in which area of London did the company open its first branch?

    A. Ealing
    B. Euston
    C. Peckham
    D. Chingford

WHERE IN THE WORLD . . . – ANSWERS

1. C – The damage to the O2's roof was so severe that it could be seen all the way from the *EastEnders* opening credits.

2. C – It was Blackpool. Boris Johnson made the most of being by the seaside with a nice gentle ~~photo op~~ jog along the coast, although Mark Francois and Rishi Sunak's plans for a day at the Pleasure Beach were thwarted by a 1.3-metre restriction on adult wristbands.

3. A – Biden was born and raised in Scranton, Pennsylvania, which is generally regarded as old-fashioned, a bit dull and of no real significance in the grand scheme of things. A good fit really.

4. A – The government struck a deal to fly asylum seekers four thousand miles to be processed in Rwanda. Net zero targets going well then.

5. B – Temperatures on Neptune dropped unexpectedly, before warming at the poles, causing havoc for people who'd booked to go there on holiday.

6. D – It was Burnley, and it was a tough challenge from a navigation point of view, as when he asked spectators which way was north, they just pointed at him.

7. B – The singer broke the bad news at the last minute, citing Covid cases and delivery delays. The cancellation forced thousands of Adele fans to scrap their trips to Vegas, coming as crushing news to local hotels, restaurants and pharmacies stocking anti-depressants.

8. C – He faked his death after paddling away from Seaton Carew on 21 March 2002. Canoeing in the sea is even more dangerous in 2022, as there's a serious risk of being shipped off to central Africa by the Home Office.

9. D – Being 'sent to Coventry' is one of the UK's most traditional threats, and is doubly grim if you add 'to watch Ed Sheeran'.

10. A – It opened in the west London district of Ealing. UK supermarkets became the latest focus of the company's supervillain-like march towards world domination, although there's a chance you bought this book from Amazon, so honestly who's to say whether it's bad or not?

NAME THAT PRIME MINISTER

Looking at Boris Johnson's popularity ratings at the end of his tenure, it seemed unfeasible that the person replacing him in office would be even more unlikeable – and yet Liz Truss decided to give it a good go. Forget the gruesome twosome that dominated 2022 by instead trying to remember the fifteen PMs that preceded them, using the dates and clues below.

1. *(2016–2019)* Unofficial fifth member of ABBA. Only lasted three years despite being a self-professed 'strong and stable' leader.
2. *(2010–2016)* Got to boss Nick Clegg around before Mark Zuckerberg did. Called the EU referendum then quit to price up sheds at B&Q.
3. *(2007–2010)* Chancellor for ten years before finally getting a go at the top job. Rather too quick to call someone a bigot.
4. *(1997–2007)* Very posh for a Labour man. Spent the early 2000s looking for WMDs.
5. *(1990–1997)* Bespectacled PM who who always looked seventy even in his forties. Partial to a Currie.
6. *(1979–1990)* First woman to lead her party and first female PM (obviously not Labour, then). Not especially popular with the mining community.

7. *(1976–1979)* The only person to have held all four Great Offices of State (Chancellor, Home Secretary, and Foreign Secretary, before becoming PM). Also holds the record for longest-living PM after reaching the ripe old age of ninety-two years, 364 days.

8. *(1974–1976)* Pipe-smoking, mac-wearing, self-styled 'man of the people' having another crack at the top job.

9. *(1970–1974)* The blue filling in a Labour sandwich, a keen yachtsman and confirmed bachelor, who installed a grand piano in No. 10.

10. *(1964–1970)* The only Labour leader to form administrations following four general elections. Assured voters that the 'pound in your pocket' would be unaffected by the devaluation of sterling.

11. *(1963–1964)* PM for a grand total of 363 days, the last to hold office while being a member of the House of Lords and, apparently, a living skeleton.

12. *(1957–1963)* One Nation Tory and Britain's last PM to have served in the First World War. Turned the sentence 'your standard of living is higher than it has been for some considerable time' into a much better slogan.

13. *(1955–1957)* Foreign Secretary for much of the Second World War – was forced to resign as PM because of an embarrassing debacle in the Middle East. Standards were different then.

14. *(1951–1955)* One of the most famous Britons in history and the only PM to receive the honour of being portrayed by Gary Oldman.

15. *(1945–1951)* Won a landslide against Churchill, despite the Second World War. First leader of a Labour majority government and introduced the NHS.

Name that Prime Minister – Answers

1. Theresa May

2. David Cameron

3. Gordon Brown

4. Tony Blair

5. John Major

6. Margaret Thatcher

7. James Callaghan

8. Harold Wilson

9. Edward Heath

10. Harold Wilson

11. Alec Douglas-Home

12. Harold Macmillan

13. Anthony Eden

14. Winston Churchill

15. Clement Attlee

Experts warned Boris Johnson that he might have been ripped off as he unveiled his prize-winning entry for the 2022 Grand National:

WHATEVER YOU DO, DON'T MENTION THE SPECIAL MILITARY OPERATION – ROUND 1

The year took a significant turn for the worse on 24 February when – after months of speculation – Russia launched a full-scale invasion of Ukraine. Can you answer these questions about the early days of the conflict?

1. Why was the meeting between Emmanuel Macron and Vladimir Putin in early February roundly ridiculed?

    A. Journalists were ordered to stand sixty feet away

    B. Macron spilled coffee on his suit

    C. They sat at opposite ends of a very long table

    D. A bird landed on Macron's lectern

2. During a press conference with Russian Foreign Minister Sergey Lavrov, then-Foreign Secretary Liz Truss said the UK would never recognise Russia's sovereignty over the Rostov and Voronezh regions. Why was this a problem?

    A. She mispronounced both regions

    B. Both are already part of Russia

    C. They are islands in the Aegean Sea

    D. They don't exist

3. US Senator Lindsey Graham caused outrage by
    calling for what?

    A. Putin to be assassinated
    B. Putin to be forgiven
    C. Russian satellites to be shot down
    D. Ukraine to surrender

4. How did former president Donald Trump suggest the
    US could attack Russia without anybody finding out?

    A. Use high-altitude drones
    B. Build a tunnel from Alaska to Russia
    C. Cover planes in Chinese flags
    D. Do it at night-time

5. Just in case the threats weren't already dramatic
    enough, what did Russia say that sanctions could lead
    to?

    A. The moon being attacked
    B. The ISS crashing to Earth
    C. Global financial collapse
    D. Earth's magnetic field shifting

6. As the war intensified, a surreal video resurfaced of
    Vladimir Putin singing which song?

    A. Blueberry Hill
    B. Bohemian Rhapsody
    C. Ace of Spades
    D. My Heart Will Go On

7. UN member states voted to condemn the invasion, although Russia, Belarus, Syria, North Korea and which other country voted against the resolution?

    A. Saudi Arabia

    B. China

    C. Eritrea

    D. Somalia

8. In early March it was revealed the UK government had approved how many visa applications for Ukrainian refugees?

    A. 10

    B. 50

    C. 250

    D. 1,000

9. In the early stages of the invasion, a Ukrainian woman was hailed a hero after destroying a Russian drone using what?

    A. A tennis ball

    B. Her fists

    C. A walking stick

    D. Tomatoes

10. After intense pressure, which global megacorporation decided to suspend operations in Russia?

    A. Pepsi

    B. McDonald's

    C. Coca-Cola

    D. All of the above

Whatever You Do, Don't Mention the Special Military Operation – Round 1 Answers

1. C – Putin's comically long tables were ridiculed as he held meetings with foreign leaders and even his own staff from about twenty feet away. It's worth noting that both Putin and Macron stand at around 5ft 7in, so from that distance they probably couldn't even see each other.

2. B – Both are cities in Russia. To make matters worse, Truss had already been mocked a week earlier for mixing up the Baltic and Black seas, though unlike her predecessor Dominic Raab, she was at least aware England is separated from mainland Europe by the sea, so there's that.

3. A – During an interview with Fox News, and then again in a tweet, the Senator for South Carolina called for someone in Putin's inner circle to step up and do the world 'a great service', although would-be snipers are skeptical about hitting him from the end of that table.

4. C – During a speech in New Orleans, Trump suggested Russian intelligence could be bamboozled with US jets disguised as Chinese ones, after taking tactical military advice from Wile E. Coyote.

5. B – A dramatic threat, but theoretically possible as Russia maintains the boosters that periodically raise the ISS. Hopefully it never happens, as surprisingly few insurance companies offer International Space Station coverage as standard.

6. A – The footage turned out to be from a 2010 charity event, and not, as previously reported, an early episode of *Tsars in their Eyes*.

7. C – It was Eritrea that joined fellow champions of human rights Belarus, Syria, North Korea and Russia itself in voting against the resolution (China abstained). In a surprising move, Jair Bolsonaro's Brazil voted in favour, although it's possible they thought they were playing Squid Game and instinctively hit the green button.

8. B – After receiving criticism for only approving fifty applications, Priti Patel proved she's not completely heartless by briefly considering a further five.

9. D – A woman in Kyiv spotted the drone from her balcony and downed it with the nearest projectile, which happened to be a jar of preserved tomatoes. Early reports wrongly claimed it was a jar of cucumbers, which just goes to show what can be lost in the fog of war.

10. D – It was indeed all three. Despite early reluctance, intense pressure on social media led to Pepsi, Coca-Cola and McDonald's ceasing operations in mainland Russia, causing life expectancy to rise by twenty years overnight.

Dodgy Tabloid Headlines

Whether they're puns, fearmongering or just down-right creepy, you can always rely on tabloid headlines to make you question the state of modern journalism, and 2022 was no exception. Can you work out what the following front pages related to?

1. I HOPE I DID YOU PROUD, MUMMY
    Sun – 11 May

    A. British fighters in Ukraine
    B. Major discovery in Egypt
    C. State opening of Parliament
    D. Toddler who called an ambulance

2. APRIL CRUEL DAY
    Mirror – 1 April

    A. Cost-of-living crisis
    B. Rise in 'mean' April Fool's pranks
    C. Priti Patel TV interview
    D. Wealthy trophy hunters

3. REBELS WITHOUT A CLUE
   Daily Mail – 1 June

   A. Russian defectors
   B. MPs joining striking rail workers
   C. Star Wars going 'woke'
   D. Backbenchers turning on Boris Johnson

4. THE HAND OF WAD
   Metro – 5 May

   A. Rishi Sunak's wife
   B. The spring budget
   C. The Pope's personal wealth
   D. A sporting auction

5. WHAT A BUNCH OF ANCHORS!
   Sun – 18 March

   A. Russian superyachts
   B. P&O Ferries
   C. The Royal Navy
   D. Extinction Rebellion

6. WAZZATHA
   Sun – 18 May

   A. Test cricket
   B. A celebrity court case
   C. Glastonbury
   D. Rise in UK drug use

7. WORLD GNAW THREE
   Daily Star – 27 May

   A. Mutant hamsters beneath London

   B. Russian dentist shortage

   C. Putin's false teeth

   D. Brits resorting to cannibalism

8. HEAR HEAR HERO
   Metro – 9 March

   A. A double ear transplant

   B. Captain Tom Moore

   C. Volodymyr Zelenskyy

   D. Pride of Britain awards

9. SHOULD'VE GONE TO SPOCKSAVERS
   Daily Star – 7 January

   A. Concerns over astronauts' eyesight

   B. Dominic Cummings

   C. A painting of Leonard Nimoy

   D. Animated *Star Trek* reboot

10. MA'AM-ALADE YOUR MAJESTY?
    Daily Mail – 5 June

    A. Food shortages

    B. Harry and Meghan

    C. Royal garden party

    D. Paddington Bear

Dodgy Tabloid Headlines – Answers

1. C – The *Sun* celebrated the seventy-three-year-old Prince Charles undertaking his first state opening of Parliament by transforming him into a toddler from the 1800s.

2. A – Energy prices went up (by a lot) on April Fool's Day, and to be fair to the government, they played along with the joke for the rest of the year by not really doing anything to help.

3. D – This was about backbenchers turning on the PM in an attempt to oust him. Not the first time Boris Johnson has been turned on of course, but it usually involves some sort of IT lesson.

4. D – Diego Maradona's shirt from the infamous 'hand of God' game at the 1986 World Cup sold for £7.1 million at auction, which as far as 2022 prices go is a pretty good deal for a T-shirt.

5. B – This one was aimed at P&O bosses after they laid off eight hundred staff without notice. When the government called upon their CEO to resign, he simply claimed he wasn't aware they were sackings and got off scot-free.

6. B – This literary masterpiece takes the concept of WAGs, then adds in Agatha and 'Wazza' for Wayne Rooney (which nobody has called him, ever) and the result is almost as unsavoury as the contents of Rebekah Vardy's WhatsApp messages.

7. D – Russian state news bizarrely claimed that Brits had resorted to eating each other. Their source? A single line from a Jeremy Clarkson article saying 'hunger makes people eat their neighbours'. It doesn't of course, but it can result in you losing your job at the BBC.

8. C – President Zelenskyy addressed the UK Parliament on the ongoing issues his country faced after being invaded by Russia. MPs briefly gave him a standing ovation before getting back to more important matters like birthday cake and curry.

9. A – A report by the Medical University of South Carolina claimed that living in space can seriously affect your eyesight. The phenomenon was first detected when an astronaut aboard the ISS hilariously thought he was looking at white dwarf HD1596894E when in reality he was looking at white dwarf HD1596894D.

10. D – The Queen appeared alongside Paddington Bear in a surprise segment during the Platinum Jubilee Concert, prompting the *Daily Mail* to question why a Peruvian migrant was handed a job that could have gone to a British bear instead.

BADLY EXPLAINED FILM PLOTS

Can you work out the following 2022 big releases from these extremely vague synopses?

1. Emotional millionaire in gimp suit faces off against flightless villain and sudoku enthusiast.
2. Garden tool-wielding loner surprisingly agile for his age.
3. Middle-aged men rediscover the joy of being kicked in the testicles.
4. Man borrows a few quid from a woman he met on a dating app. Man borrows a few quid from a woman he met on a dating app. Man borrows a few quid from a woman he met on a dating app (repeat ad infinitum).
5. Flying woman gets over the death of her boyfriend by mucking about in different realities with a sexy wizard.
6. Spiky collector of precious metals and his yellow mate get roughed up by an angry red bloke.
7. Head teacher teams up with a magic zookeeper to battle not-Johnny Depp.
8. Dysfunctional upper-class family are dusted off and sent on a package holiday to the south of France.
9. Middle-aged vampire unlikely to be recruited by the Avengers.
10. Life finds a way . . . to flog a dead horse.

Badly Explained Film Plots – Answers

1. *The Batman*

2. *Texas Chainsaw Massacre*

3. *Jackass Forever*

4. *The Tinder Swindler*

5. *Doctor Strange in the Multiverse of Madness*

6. *Sonic the Hedgehog 2*

7. *Fantastic Beasts: The Secrets of Dumbledore*

8. *Downton Abbey: A New Era*

9. *Morbius*

10. *Jurassic World Dominion*

Sequel to *Day of the Triffids* 'not in the works'
said movie execs, after a misleading sign appeared
in a village near Manchester:

2022 General Knowledge – Round 1

Here are ten questions that we couldn't shoehorn into other rounds so we bundled them together in the name of fun.

1. In June, what did TV presenter Kirstie Allsopp reveal she'd accidentally eaten?

   A. A fly
   B. Nettles
   C. An Apple AirPod
   D. Her wedding ring

2. During a chess tournament in Moscow over the summer, a seven-year-old boy was playing against an automated robot when what happened?

   A. The robot broke into song
   B. It flipped the board and stormed off
   C. It exploded
   D. It broke the boy's finger

3. The Lib Dems overturned a Tory majority of 24,200 to pull off a stunning by-election win in which constituency?

    A. Torridge and West Devon
    B. Newton Abbot
    C. Tiverton and Honiton
    D. Exeter

4. Which Spice Girl joined Blossoms onstage at Glastonbury for a rousing rendition of 'Spice Up Your Life'?

    A. Sporty
    B. Ginger
    C. Scary
    D. Baby

5. During the Select Committee hearings into the 6 January Capitol attack, Donald Trump's former press secretary Stephanie Grisham revealed that when he lost his temper, staff would calm him down by playing a song from which musical?

    A. *West Side Story*
    B. *Cats*
    C. *Starlight Express*
    D. *Les Misérables*

6. In one of the more peculiar cultural events of the year, 10 March marked the seventh annual celebration of which video game character?

    A. Mario

    B. Pac-Man

    C. Sonic the Hedgehog

    D. Lara Croft

7. In May, a married couple from Gloucester won a record-breaking £184 million EuroMillions jackpot. What was the first thing they bought with their newfound wealth?

    A. A ride-on lawnmower

    B. Their own caravan park

    C. Some more lottery tickets

    D. A second-hand Volvo

8. While standing in at PMQs for Boris Johnson (who was at the G7 summit), Dominic Raab called Angela Rayner a 'champagne socialist' for attending what?

    A. The opera

    B. Royal Ascot

    C. The Proms

    D. Gardeners' World Live

9. Throughout 2022, a steady stream of photographs of Ryan Gosling and Margot Robbie routinely broke the internet as they shot scenes dressed as which iconic couple?

    A. Sid and Nancy
    B. Romeo and Juliet
    C. Homer and Marge
    D. Barbie and Ken

10. Many, many people were defrauded of their NFTs in 2022, but why was actor Seth Green especially devastated when it happened to him?

    A. It resold for twice what he paid
    B. He had to cancel a TV show
    C. It was stolen by a close friend
    D. He'd only owned it for fifteen minutes

2022 General Knowledge – Round 1 Answers

1. C – Kirstie Allsopp claimed she'd swallowed one of her AirPods along with a handful of vitamins, possibly after misunderstanding the concept of an apple a day keeping the doctor away.

2. D – The robot grabbed the boy's finger and broke it. Officials at the Russian event played down the incident before quietly deploying the robot to Ukraine as a makeshift general.

3. C – The Lib Dems pulled off a huge swing to win the Tiverton and Honiton by-election, although the party atmosphere came to an abrupt end when Ed Davey arrived with one of his trademark tacky props to gurn next to – this time a big blue door with 'It's time to show Boris Johnson the door' spray-painted on the front.

4. A – Sporty Spice, aka Mel C, joined Blossoms onstage at Glastonbury. Incidentally, police reported a huge drop in drug-related offences at this year's festival, so spicing up your life was actually incredibly difficult.

5. B – It was the song 'Memory' from *Cats*, which Grisham said would be played by a member of staff known as 'the Music Man' to calm the president. Failing that, they'd place a tea towel over his head to make him think it was night time.

6. A – Mario Day has steadily grown in popularity in the UK since 2016, despite warnings from Nigel Farage that we shouldn't teach children to glorify manual labourers from Italy.

7. D – Joe and Jess Thwaite revealed they forked out £38,000 of their £184 million on a second-hand Volvo estate, and after filling it with fuel they still had more than £40 million left in the bank.

8. A – Raab called Angela Rayner a champagne socialist after she had the audacity to attend a performance of *The Marriage of Figaro* at Glyndebourne. Rayner responded by saying 'never let anyone tell you you're not good enough', unless of course you're the Labour Party during the last three general elections.

9. D – They were filming scenes for *Barbie*, which is set to be released in 2023. To prepare for the role of Ken, Ryan Gosling went full method by painting his crotch blue and amputating his penis.

10. B – Seth Green had to halt production of animated comedy *White Horse Tavern* as it was based around his Bored Ape NFT, which was then stolen and sold on for $200,000. Comedy or no comedy, at least everyone got a laugh out of it.

ALLOW ME TO INTRODUCE MYSELF

The following people all appeared as panellists on *Have I Got News for You* in 2022, but can you work out who they are from the host's introduction?

1. 'A Labour MP who voted for Moldova in the European Song Contest. She also voted for Keir Starmer as leader. I mean, principles are fine, but would it hurt you to back a winner once in a while?'

    A. Lisa Nandy
    B. Jess Phillips
    C. Emily Thornberry
    D. Diane Abbott

2. 'A journalist who recently said leaving the BBC for Channel 4 was the best decision she has ever made. Well, look who's come crawling back.'

    A. Steph McGovern
    B. Cathy Newman
    C. Jackie Long
    D. Fatima Manji

3. 'A BBC journalist described by *The Times* as having a voice that would sound soothing announcing the apocalypse. He's taken a break from rehearsing that to be here.'

   A. Clive Myrie

   B. Huw Edwards

   C. Justin Webb

   D. John Simpson

4. 'A professor of mathematics at UCL who teaches her students how to work with astronomical numbers. This week she's been helping them deal with the new interest rates on their student loans.'

   A. Joanna Verran

   B. Maggie Aderin-Pocock

   C. Hannah Fry

   D. Ruth Lawrence

5. 'A writer and broadcaster who says of quizzes that he's really competitive but he doesn't mind losing. If only we'd known earlier, we'd have put him on Ian's team.'

   A. Richard Coles

   B. Alexander Armstrong

   C. Phillip Schofield

   D. Richard Osman

6. 'On Paul's team tonight is a broadcaster and Labour peer who says that the best advice she ever received was from her mother, who told her "Life's unfair, get used to it". I couldn't agree more, so it's two points to Ian's team.'

    A. Gillian Merron
    B. Martha Osamor
    C. Shami Chakrabarti
    D. Joan Bakewell

7. 'A man who loves intricate pieces of machinery, which he studies for hours to see exactly how they work, so to save him some time, this ... [points to set backboards as they spin] ... is literally a bloke pulling a lever.'

    A. Ross Noble
    B. James May
    C. Joe Lycett
    D. Michael Portillo

8. 'A journalist who once wrote an article called "What happens when a joke is followed by silence?" As Chris Rock can testify, it's not the worst thing that can happen.'

    A. Stacey Dooley
    B. Sophie Raworth
    C. Helen Lewis
    D. Rachel Johnson

9. 'A political journalist who has recently become a new father. It's hard; they sleep all day, only waking up to scream and demand food, but sometimes they help with the baby.'

    A. Tim Shipman

    B. Sam Coates

    C. Robert Peston

    D. Andrew Marr

10. 'A comedian who originally trained as an electrician – and with the massive increase in energy bills, we're already grateful to her for wiring up the studio to the next-door hospital's dialysis machine.'

    A. Sara Pascoe

    B. Zoe Lyons

    C. Susie McCabe

    D. Ania Magliano

ALLOW ME TO INTRODUCE MYSELF – ANSWERS

1. **B** – Jess Phillips

2. **A** – Steph McGovern

3. **C** – Justin Webb

4. **C** – Hannah Fry

5. **D** – Richard Osman

6. **D** – Joan Bakewell

7. **B** – James May

8. **C** – Helen Lewis

9. **A** – Tim Shipman

10. **C** – Susie McCabe

Nigel Farage's struggle for post-Brexit relevancy
continued in 2022, despite his rendition of 'Nessun
dorma' earning a golden buzzer from Amanda Holden:

FILMED ON FAUX-CATION

In 2022 it was revealed people don't need good neighbours after all, as the long-running soap was cancelled after thirty-seven years. Although everyone knows it took place in Ramsay Street, true fans will know it was set in the non-existent suburb of Erinsborough. Below are the names of ten other TV shows, but can you identify the fictional places in which they're set?

1. *Coronation Street*

   A. Weatherfield
   B. Werrington
   C. Wethersby
   D. Weatherford

2. *The Bill*

   A. Winstanton
   B. Moon Crescent
   C. Sun Hill
   D. Hill View

3. *Grange Hill*

   A. Wylesly
   B. Northam
   C. Gristleford
   D. Costington

4. *Fireman Sam*

    A. Pintyponty

    B. Pandypootle

    C. Puntypanto

    D. Pontypandy

5. *EastEnders*

    A. Walton

    B. Warford

    C. Wharfdale

    D. Walford

6. *Noel's House Party*

    A. Creaky Backside

    B. Crinkley Bottom

    C. Creamy Buttocks

    D. Crispy Bumcheek

7. *Footballers' Wives*

    A. Grestley

    B. Burstall

    C. Earls Park

    D. Park End

8. *Postman Pat*

    A. Greenvale
    B. Vale Green
    C. Bowlers' Green
    D. Greendale

9. *Home and Away*

    A. Summer Bay
    B. Sunshine Cove
    C. Sunnydale
    D. Sun Valley

10. *Thomas the Tank Engine*

    A. Sodley
    B. Sodor
    C. Sodom
    D. Gomorrah

Filmed on Faux-cation – Answers

1. A – *Coronation Street* is the world's longest-running television soap opera and takes place in the fictional northern town of **Weatherfield**. As of 2022 there have been more than 10,700 episodes, most of which focus on typical working-class scenarios like going to the pub, having affairs and being killed by an out-of-control tram.

2. C – *The Bill* was set in **Sun Hill** and was axed six months after David Cameron became Prime Minister – presumably after sweeping cuts to the constabulary.

3. B – *Grange Hill* was set in the fictional London borough of **Northam**, and left fans devastated when it ended after thirty years without explaining who threw that sausage during the opening credits.

4. D – *Fireman Sam* takes place in the peaceful Welsh village of **Pontypandy**, which easily has the highest number of fires per capita anywhere in the UK, and for connoisseurs of cultural insensitivity, the village's only Italian resident is called Bella Lasagne.

5. D – Home of the depressing Christmas episode, *EastEnders* is set in the fictional London borough of **Walford**, where people are 95 per cent more likely than the average cockney to be brutally murdered during the month of December.

6. B – **Crinkley Bottom** was the setting for *Noel's House Party*, which in 2010 was voted the best Saturday night TV show of all time, ahead of *The X Factor* and *Strictly Come Dancing*. Such was the popularity of the show that it spawned not one but three Crinkley Bottom amusement parks, which were a roaring success for at least three bank holidays before going out of business in 1997.

7. **C** – *Footballers' Wives (2002 – 2006)* was set in **Earls Park** and consisted mostly of glamour models having sex with Gary Lucy, with the odd football reference thrown in here and there to let him get his breath back.

8. **D** – *Postman Pat* is set in the village of **Greendale**, and follows the exploits of Pat Clifton, who has managed to keep his job for forty-one years despite losing almost every parcel that ever had the misfortune of being in his bright red van. The series took a dark turn in 2003 when sub-postmistress Mrs Goggins was handed a six-year prison sentence on the basis of faulty accounting software.

9. **A** – **Summer Bay** is the setting for *Home and Away*, which is almost completely indistinguishable from *Neighbours* except for the fact it's got a slightly less annoying theme song and is actually still on the telly.

10. **B** – *Thomas the Tank Engine* is set on the Island of **Sodor**, where a group of anthropomorphic trains bow to the will of the Fat Controller, who was later rebranded to Sir Topham Hatt after receiving a knighthood and a gastric band.

BADLY TRANSLATED QUOTES OF 2022 – ROUND 1

The following are all 2022 quotes from politicians and celebrities ... with a twist. They've been back and forth through Google Translate a few times, making them either more or less intelligible, depending on who originally said it.

1. 'As Rafiki in the king of lions, change is yes, and very big the change ... yes? but oh no.'

    A.   Rishi Sunak
    B.   Jess Phillips
    C.   Boris Johnson
    D.   Lisa Nandy

2. 'I gave in because very close and worrisome, dangerous. The rules they were lost but it was good illegal don't talk about this.'

    A.   Matt Hancock
    B.   John Bercow
    C.   Jeremy Corbyn
    D.   Dominic Cummings

3. 'If we have clothes on and an bus to drive to game, we would be there and competition very hard.'

    A. Jürgen Klopp

    B. Antonio Conte

    C. Thomas Tuchel

    D. Gareth Southgate

4. 'I have completely not going and I believe that I'm having been totally for the last five years, being a genuine metamorphosis in the meet.'

    A. Sadiq Khan

    B. Cressida Dick

    C. John Major

    D. John Prescott

5. 'Kanye is has become toadying, wolflike, very bad the shocking jockey and I not laugh.'

    A. Holly Willoughby

    B. Richard Madeley

    C. Kim Kardashian

    D. Piers Morgan

6. 'We have talk regarding what more punish yes hopefully. We're very clear the crank crank useless the crank.'

    A. Emmanuel Macron
    B. Olaf Scholz
    C. Dominic Raab
    D. Liz Truss

7. 'Damon all bran I was very a big appreciate of yours until I view this. I written ALL my song.'

    A. Billie Eilish
    B. Liam Gallagher
    C. Taylor Swift
    D. Lewis Capaldi

8. 'I would like write down fifty six players who I think should no more time play men united. Only shame, the big shame.'

    A. Roy Keane
    B. Jamie Carragher
    C. Gary Neville
    D. Micah Richards

9. 'Did my right heroic companion had not reading rules or did not he understand the meaning and others surround him, or they did not think rule apply? Number 10 the choosing?'

    A. Angela Rayner

    B. Theresa May

    C. Peter Bone

    D. Bill Cash

10. 'When I buy my first become the owning of, go abroad, the easy jet, the coffee and gym Netflix . . . it not so much.'

    A. Denise Welch

    B. Alan Sugar

    C. Martin Lewis

    D. Kirsty Allsopp

Badly Translated Quotes of 2022 – Round 1 Answers

1. C – 'As Rafiki in *The Lion King* says, change is good, and change is necessary even though it's tough.' – Boris Johnson adopting a more mature tone (well, more mature than that time he wouldn't stop talking about Peppa Pig World) after several members of staff quit at the height of the so-called 'partygate' scandal.

Independent – 4 February

2. A – 'I resigned because I broke the social-distancing guidelines. By then, they weren't actually rules, they weren't the law. But that's not the point.' – Matt Hancock on the *Diary of a CEO* podcast, despite being neither a CEO or someone capable of writing a diary.

Diary of a CEO podcast – 28 February

3. C – 'As long as we have enough shirts and a bus to drive to the games, we'll be there and will compete hard.' – Thomas Tuchel kept his head up as news broke that Chelsea owner Roman Abramovich had been sanctioned. Thankfully the team had an abundance of spare shirts, as they couldn't currently sell any in the club shop.

Eurosport – 10 March

4. B – 'I have absolutely no intention of going and I believe that I am and have been, actually for the last five years, leading a real transformation in the Met.' – Cressida Dick putting her foot down to say she wasn't going anywhere, and she was right, for about another two hours.

Glasgow Times – 10 February

5. D – 'Kanye's become a sneering, snarling, shambolic shock-jock and none of it makes me laugh.' – Piers Morgan took exception to Kanye West being an outspoken, shameless attention-seeker, presumably on copyright grounds.

Sun – 14 February

6. D – 'We discussed what more sanctions we can put on. We're very clear the ratchet needs to be tightened.' – Liz Truss on potential further sanctions to scare Russia – not least the prospect of further discussions with Liz Truss.

Telegraph – 11 March

7. C – 'Damon Albarn I was such a big fan of yours until I saw this. I write ALL of my own songs.' – Taylor Swift after the Blur frontman questioned her song-writing credentials. Swift fans questioned whether he'd ever actually listened to her songs, as the last thing you want as a bloke is to be in Taylor Swift's bad books.

Twitter – 24 January

8. A – 'I could write down five or six players who I think should never play for Man United again. Just shameful, shameful.' – Roy Keane after Manchester United's 4–1 defeat to Manchester City – thankfully for non-Man U fans and comedy fans alike, the players Keane singled out would continue to 'play' for the rest of the season.

Metro – 6 March

9. B – 'Either my right honourable friend had not read the rules or didn't understand what they meant and others around him, or they didn't think the rules applied to No. 10. Which was it?' – Theresa May moments before becoming the 12,487th person to be told to wait until the publication of the full Sue Gray report.

Independent – 31 January

10. D – 'When I bought my first property, going abroad, the easyJet, coffee, gym, Netflix lifestyle didn't exist.' – Kirsty Allsopp on young people claiming they can't afford property. The comments led to thousands of young people cancelling their Netflix subscriptions and using the money to buy five-bed townhouses in Knightsbridge.

The Times – 6 February

CROSSWORDLE

Wordle took the world by storm in 2022. Can you solve the below crossword made up of five-letter answers that featured in the last twelve months?

Across

1. Informal noun for a man. Someone you might see down the pub.

3. Common name for currency used in numerous countries including Nepal, Mauritius and the Seychelles.

5. Ancient code system where words or phrases are represented by something else, such as letters or symbols. Also the surname of an Ian Rankin character.

9. Formally, an adjective for good judgement. Informally, someone in the north thinks you're pleasant.

10. A very, very strong type of adhesive.

11. Method of frying food in fat. Also a type of ballet jump.

15. Often found in a gun but not particularly lethal. Used to seal gaps.

16. Apparatus used to cook food.

17. A type of horse, and also a place where Hobbits live.

Down

2. Stage of an insect's life that occurs between egg and pupa (singular).

4. The authority to represent another person, especially in voting. For IT buffs, it's also a type of server.

6. Salty water used to preserve food.

7. To grimace at something shocking or disgusting.

8. Something recognisable as a significant or recurrent theme, particularly in the arts.

9. A person with a tendency to doubt sincerity in others.

11. A group of people, particularly in sports or the military. Taylor Swift has one.

12. Something that is understood without being expressed directly.

13. A word used to describe the movement and sound of water. Informally it can mean to punch someone.

14. A binary compound of oxygen, but more importantly one half of a 90s garage duo who reached number one in April 2000 with 'Bound 4 Da Reload'.

CrossWordle – Answers

Across

1. BLOKE *(Wordle #250)*
3. RUPEE *(Wordle #255)*
5. REBUS *(Wordle #196)*
9. CANNY *(Wordle #323)*
10. EPOXY *(Wordle #280)*
11. SAUTE *(Wordle #272)*
15. CAULK *(Wordle #242)*
16. STOVE *(Wordle #284)*
17. SHIRE *(Wordle #212)*

Down

2. LARVA *(Wordle #315)*
4. PROXY *(Wordle #213)*
6. BRINE *(Wordle #259)*
7. WINCE *(Wordle #217)*
8. TROPE *(Wordle #287)*
9. CYNIC *(Wordle #240)*
11. SQUAD *(Wordle #296)*
12. TACIT *(Wordle #246)*
13. SLOSH *(Wordle #276)*
14. OXIDE *(Wordle #306)*

At the Grand National there was a sad moment as three horses had to be destroyed at the same time:

MISSING WORDS – ROUND 1

If there's one thing 2022 wasn't short of, it was bizarre headlines, but can you fill in the blanks?

1. 'Drowned woman' turns out to be _____
    The Week – 10 February

    A. Headless sex doll
    B. Anne Summers mannequin
    C. CPR dummy
    D. Clump of seaweed

2. Primark teams up with _____ for exclusive clothing range
    You magazine – 16 February

    A. Wrights Pies
    B. Pret a Manger
    C. Wimpy
    D. Greggs

3. Waitrose to stock the UK's first _____ onions from next month
    Daily Record – 12 January

    A. Blue
    B. Rectangular
    C. Chocolate-covered
    D. Tearless

4. Mum with 'Britain's biggest _____' doesn't
   care what trolls think
   Liverpool Echo – 1 March

   A. Front lawn
   B. Eyebrows
   C. Feet
   D. Fingernails

5. Winter Olympian suffers 'unbearably' painful
   _____ after cross-country skiing race
   Sky News – 21 February

   A. Ruptured testicle
   B. Frozen penis
   C. Icy diarrhoea
   D. Chafed nipples

6. Florida man arrested after stealing a _____ by
   stuffing it down his trousers
   Sky News – 24 February

   A. Pelican
   B. Bike
   C. Crossbow
   D. Crocodile

7. _____ deployed in New Zealand to repel Covid protesters
   NME – 13 February

    A.   Wild boar
    B.   'The brown note'
    C.   Wasps
    D.   James Blunt's music

8. Elon Musk offers teenager $5,000 to stop _____
   LADbible – 27 January

    A.   Tracking his private jet
    B.   Sending him pictures of Shrek
    C.   Giving out his phone number
    D.   Calling him 'Elrond Tusk'

9. London posties stagger around after accidentally

   _____
   Metro – 3 February

    A.   Inhaling laughing gas
    B.   Drinking whisky
    C.   Consuming magic mushrooms
    D.   Eating a load of hash brownies

10. Perfume with _____ scent sells out within
    hours
    New York Post – 14 February

    A.   Baked beans
    B.   Wood shavings
    C.   French fries
    D.   Egg

MISSING WORDS – ROUND 1 ANSWERS

1. A – '"Drowned woman" turns out to be **headless sex doll**.' The sixty-seven-year-old man who 'rescued' the doll says the penny dropped when he performed CPR and water spurted from three different holes.

2. D – 'Primark teams up with **Greggs** for exclusive clothing range.' The collaboration nobody asked for was surprisingly popular, with clothes available in a range of sizes from XXL to XXXXXL.

3. D – 'Waitrose to stock the UK's first **tearless** onions from next month.' Worth noting however that the no-crying bit only applies to chopping, and not the moment you realise you paid £78.56 for three onions.

4. B – 'Mum with "Britain's biggest **eyebrows**" doesn't care what trolls think.' A twenty-seven-year-old mum from Grimsby made headlines with painted-on eyebrows that cover nearly half of her forehead. Although claiming to be indifferent to the reaction, her expression appears to be a mixture of happy, sad, shocked, frightened and curious.

5. B – 'Winter Olympian suffers "unbearably" painful **frozen penis** after cross-country skiing race.' After suffering the horrific injury, Finnish athlete Remi Lindholm says he knew it had thawed when he suddenly piste himself.

6. C – 'Man arrested after stealing a **crossbow** by stuffing it down his trousers.' A forty-six-year-old man walked into a store in Brevard County, Florida, concealed the weapon in his clothes and walked out. Staff at the store say they had suspicions he was stealing a crossbow when he suddenly made a bolt for it (copyright *The Two Ronnies*, 1978).

7. D – '**James Blunt's music** deployed in New Zealand to repel Covid protesters.' Doctors criticised the move however after several people were admitted to hospital with . . . Blunt force trauma. Sorry.

8. A – 'Elon Musk offers teenager $5,000 to stop **tracking his private jet.**' Nineteen-year-old teenager Jack Sweeney developed a Twitter bot that posted updates on Elon Musk's whereabouts, which was hugely helpful as it meant people could ensure they were never at risk of being near Elon Musk.

9. D – 'London posties stagger around after accidentally eating **a load of hash brownies**.' Royal Mail launched an investigation after staff reportedly ate brownies they found in an unclaimed package. A perfectly normal response, of course, to discover something brown and sticky in a random parcel and think 'looks tasty, I'll eat that'.

10. C – 'Perfume with **French fries** scent sells out within hours.' Presumably snapped up by the same people who bought a Greggs jumper.

CLUB CRAWL

The following footballers all played at the top level in 2022, but can you identify them from just their club history?*

(* Excludes loan deals)

1. Sporting CP *(2002–2003)*, Manchester United *(2003–2009)*, Real Madrid *(2009–2018)*, Juventus *(2018–2021)*, Manchester United *(2021– present)*.

2. Anderlecht *(2009–2011)*, Chelsea *(2011–2014)*, Everton *(2014–2017)*, Manchester United *(2017–2019)*, Inter Milan *(2019–2021)*, Chelsea *(2021– present)*.

3. Al Mokawloon *(2010–2012)*, Basel *(2012–2014)*, Chelsea *(2014–2016)*, Roma *(2016–2017)*, Liverpool *(2017– present)*.

4. Stocksbridge Park Steels *(2007–2010)*, Halifax Town *(2010–2011)*, Fleetwood Town *(2011–2012)*, Leicester City *(2012– present)*.

5. Southampton *(2005–2006)*, Arsenal *(2006–2018)*, Everton *(2018–2021)*, Southampton *(2021– present)*.

6. Lumezzane *(2006)*, Inter Milan *(2007–2010)*, Manchester City *(2010–2013)*, AC Milan *(2013–2014)*, Liverpool *(2014–2016)*, Nice *(2016–2019)*, Marseille *(2019)*, Brescia *(2019–2020)*, Monza *(2020–2021)*, Adana Demirspor *(2021– present)*.

7. Nacional *(2005–2006)*, Groningen *(2006–2007)*, Ajax *(2007–2011)*, Liverpool *(2011–2014)*, Barcelona *(2014–2020)*, Atlético Madrid *(2020– present)*.

8. Sunderland *(2002–2007)*, Leeds United *(2007–2010)*, Arsenal *(2010–2013)*, Manchester City *(2014– present)*.

9. West Ham United *(2004–2022)*.

10. Malmö *(1999–2001)*, Ajax *(2001–2004)*, Juventus *(2004–2006)*, Inter Milan *(2006–2009)*, Barcelona *(2009–2011)*, AC Milan *(2011–2012)*, Paris Saint-Germain *(2012–2016)*, Manchester United *(2016–2018)*, LA Galaxy *(2018–2019)*, AC Milan *(2020– present)*.

Club Crawl — Answers

1. Cristiano Ronaldo

2. Romelu Lukaku

3. Mo Salah

4. Jamie Vardy

5. Theo Walcott

6. Mario Balotelli

7. Luis Suárez

8. Steph Houghton

9. Mark Noble

10. Zlatan Ibrahimović

A keen astronomer in West London tracked the orbit of
Kepa Arrizabalaga's 2022 League Cup final penalty:

LONDON'S HOTTEST PARTY VENUE – PART 1

For most people, the lockdowns of 2020 and 2021 consisted of sitting in the kitchen, watching Netflix and not having the heart to tell your boss they were on mute. However, reports from Downing Street this year suggested that for some, those hazy days had resembled a Magaluf booze cruise. Unsurprisingly the general public wasn't entirely happy about it . . .

1. As Boris Johnson faced increasing pressure over parties at No. 10, which fellow golden-haired MP came rushing to his defence, arguing that the 'circumstances' of working in Downing Street were different to those of other workplaces across Britain?

    A. Michael Fabricant
    B. Tom Tugendhat
    C. Oliver Dowden
    D. Grant Shapps

2. Ahead of a fiery PMQs on 19 January, Conservative MP Christian Wakeford shocked his party by doing what?

    A. He resigned
    B. He arrived at PMQs wearing shorts
    C. He defected to Labour
    D. He admitted attending parties at No. 10

3. In the same session, which Tory MP broke ranks and publicly called for Boris Johnson to resign?

   A. Mark Francois

   B. Theresa May

   C. Peter Bone

   D. David Davis

4. And in doing so, they quoted Oliver Cromwell by telling the PM . . .

   A. By the grace of God, go!

   B. In the name of God, go!

   C. For the love of God, go!

   D. Begone, vile beast!

5. Downing Street staff reportedly used what to discreetly transport party supplies into No. 10?

   A. A suitcase

   B. A washing basket

   C. A Ford Transit van

   D. Rishi Sunak's wallet

6. One of the parties investigated by Sue Gray took place on the day Dominic Cummings left No. 10, and was said to be themed around which band?

   A. The Beach Boys

   B. Fleetwood Mac

   C. AC/DC

   D. ABBA

7. Which MP was ejected from the Commons after refusing to retract comments that Boris Johnson had misled Parliament over lockdown parties?

    A.   Ian Blackford

    B.   Angela Eagle

    C.   Jess Phillips

    D.   Ed Davey

8. As evidence of Downing Street lockdown parties began to stack up, Boris Johnson claimed that they were in fact what?

    A.   Training sessions

    B.   Team-building exercises

    C.   Work events

    D.   Conferences

9. During one reportedly boozy session on 16 April 2021, revellers were said to have broken what in the Downing Street garden?

    A.   A statue of Winston Churchill

    B.   A ceramic pot

    C.   A patio table

    D.   A swing

10. Sue Gray's (heavily redacted) report was finally released on 31 January. How many of the sixteen gatherings were revealed to be under police investigation?

    A.   8

    B.   10

    C.   12

    D.   14

LONDON'S HOTTEST PARTY VENUE – PART 1
ANSWERS

1. A – Fabricant was one of several MPs sent out on the media rounds to defend the PM, marking a harrowing period for children (and their parents) as he was often shown on TV before the watershed.

2. C – Christian Wakeford, MP for Bury South, decided to instead bury his career and crossed the floor to join Labour. The fact that you probably thought 'Christian who?' means the UK's political landscape just about survived this seismic shift.

3. D – It was former Brexit Secretary David Davis. The initial reaction in the Commons was that of shock, which quickly turned to confusion as MPs tried to work out whether losing the confidence of David Davis was good or bad.

4. B – At the time it was unclear how Boris Johnson's premiership could possibly survive such a scathing attack, until a few minutes later, when it easily did.

5. A – When challenged, the Met said officers at No. 10 are there to prevent terror attacks, and not to 'check what's in people's bags', which makes sense because terrorists famously never hide things in bags.

6. D – It was ABBA (who, ironically would go on to release 'I Still Have Faith in You' a few months later). The party was said to be a celebration of Dominic Cummings's departure, which even Boris Johnson's harshest critics have to admit is fair enough.

7. A – Blackford's ejection marked a harrowing forty-five minutes for the Scottish National Party leader, as he received no attention whatsoever while he power-walked across London to Speakers' Corner.

8. C – Johnson described the gatherings as 'work events', and said that everything looked completely above board from his position in the conga line.

9. D – Several sources claimed a baby swing belonging to the Prime Minister's son was broken. Rishi Sunak was quick to point out that it couldn't have been him, as being four inches shorter than Wilfred it would have comfortably supported his weight.

10. C – The handful of words that were published in Sue Gray's initial report didn't reveal a great deal, but they did confirm twelve parties (that weren't parties) were being investigated by the police. The Russian invasion of Ukraine would take the heat off Boris Johnson for a short while, but this story was far from over.

Odd One Out – Round 1

A familiar *Have I Got News for You* round: four things, but which one doesn't belong?

1.

A: Roy Keane

B: Snow White

C: Ronnie O'Sullivan

D: Michael Schumacher

2.

A: Sir Isaac Newton

B: Guy Fawkes

C: Sebastian Coe

D: Nancy Astor

ODD ONE OUT – ROUND 1 ANSWERS

1. B – Snow White is the odd one out. Keane, Schumacher and O'Sullivan have all won something seven times (Keane – Premier League titles, Schumacher – F1 titles, O'Sullivan – Snooker World Championships) whereas Snow White's only connection to the number seven is her dubious living arrangement with a gang of dwarves.

2. B – Guy Fawkes is the odd one out. Newton, Coe and Astor were all MPs easily distracted by other interests, whereas Fawkes was – in his attempt to blow up Parliament – a highly focused and committed fanatic.

In Moscow, there was a tense stand-off as employees worked up the courage to tell the boss he was on mute:

WE'RE NOT WORTHY!

Glastonbury 2022 saw fans return to Worthy Farm for the first time since 2019 owing to cancellations during the pandemic, but can you work out which of the following are real acts that played at this year's festival and which are completely made up?

1. Wet Leg
2. 60ft Traffic Warden
3. House of Cheese
4. Beabadoobee
5. Bicep
6. Slug Pellet Massacre
7. Camel Torpedo
8. Amyl and The Sniffers
9. Insecure Colin
10. First Aid Kit
11. Jiggles and Beans
12. Dirty Forceps
13. Snarky Puppy
14. Doctor Wolfman and the Full Moons
15. Spaghetti Bolognese
16. Confidence Man
17. Big Thief
18. Kent Astrological Society
19. Window Cleaner
20. Dry Cleaning

21. The Sex Pests
22. Greentea Peng
23. The Lappy Mondays ft: Chaz Robertson
24. The Unquenchable Thirst
25. Nightmares on Wax
26. Self Esteem
27. Paul, Paul, Paul, Paul, Paul, Steve and Paul
28. Turnstile
29. Squid
30. Nigella Lawson's Vintage Wok

WE'RE NOT WORTHY! – ANSWERS

Real	Not Real
1. Wet Leg	**2.** 60ft Traffic Warden
4. Beabadoobee	**3.** House of Cheese
5. Bicep	**6.** Slug Pellet Massacre
8. Amyl and The Sniffers	**7.** Camel Torpedo
10. First Aid Kit	**9.** Insecure Colin
13. Snarky Puppy	**11.** Jiggles and Beans
16. Confidence Man	**12.** Dirty Forceps
17. Big Thief	**14.** Doctor Wolfman and the Full Moons
20. Dry Cleaning	**15.** Spaghetti Bolognese
22. Greentea Peng	**18.** Kent Astrological Society
25. Nightmares on Wax	**19.** Window Cleaner
26. Self Esteem	**21.** The Sex Pests
28. Turnstile	**23.** The Lappy Mondays ft: Chaz Robertson
29. Squid	**24.** The Unquenchable Thirst
	27. Paul, Paul, Paul, Paul, Paul, Steve and Paul
	30. Nigella Lawson's Vintage Wok

ORDER! ORDER!

This one's simple (to explain at least). Can you arrange the following lists – all related to 2022 – into the correct order?

1. One of the following places was awarded city status in 2022, but can you arrange them chronologically by the year they became cities?

   A. Wolverhampton
   B. Southend-on-Sea
   C. Chelmsford
   D. Chichester

2. 2022 saw rock veterans Red Hot Chili Peppers announce a new tour and album. Can you arrange these other still-touring bands by the year in which they formed (oldest to most recent)?

   A. U2
   B. Kiss
   C. Metallica
   D. Aerosmith

3. Arrange the following countries into the order they appeared on the 2022 World Happiness Report (happiest to least happy).

   A. United Kingdom
   B. Israel
   C. Finland
   D. Germany

4. The following MPs have extremely long continuous service in the Commons, but do you know in which order they rank (shortest to longest time served)?

   A. Sir Peter Bottomley (Con)
   B. Sir Edward Leigh (Con)
   C. Harriet Harman (Lab)
   D. Barry Sheerman (Lab)

5. In 2022 work got underway on Thorpe Park's new roller coaster, which is set to be the tallest in the UK when it opens in 2024 – but can you arrange the UK's current tallest coasters by height (smallest to largest)?

   A. Stealth (Thorpe Park)
   B. The Odyssey (Fantasy Island)
   C. The Big One (Blackpool Pleasure Beach)
   D. Millennium (Fantasy Island)

6. Sort the following racehorses by the order in which they finished in the 2022 Grand National (best-placed finisher first)

    A. Lostintranslation (50-1)
    B. Noble Yeats (50-1)
    C. Delta Work (10–1)
    D. Any Second Now (15–2)

7. Arrange the following countries by smallest to largest population. (As of print date. Also assuming Russia hasn't nuked humanity into oblivion and you're not reading a charred copy of this book in a bunker forty years from now.)

    A. Russia
    B. United Kingdom
    C. Greenland
    D. Nigeria

8. The following sporting events from 2022 all drew massive crowds, but can you sort them by number of fans in attendance (least to most)?

    A. League Cup Final – Chelsea vs Liverpool
    B. F1 Australian Grand Prix (Race day only)
    C. Six Nations – England vs Wales
    D. Super Bowl LVI – Cincinnati Bengals vs LA Rams

9. The Queen celebrated a record-breaking seventy years on the throne in 2022, but can you sort these other British monarchs by length of reign (longest to shortest)?

   A. George III
   B. Edward VIII
   C. Victoria
   D. William IV

10. One of 2022's biggest box office smashes was *Toy Story* spin-off *Lightyear*, but can you arrange these other Pixar titles by the year in which they were released (oldest to most recent)?

   A. *The Incredibles*
   B. *WALL-E*
   C. *A Bug's Life*
   D. *Coco*

ORDER! ORDER! – ANSWERS

1. D, A, C, B – Southend-on-Sea became the UK's newest city on 1 March 2022. Chelmsford was proclaimed a city in 2012, Wolverhampton in 2001 and Chichester all the way back in 1075, meaning 'weekend city break in Stoke' retained its title as most depressing phrase in the English language.

2. D, B, A, C – Aerosmith is the oldest of this bunch, having formed in 1970 (Kiss – 1973, U2 – 1978, Metallica – 1981). Regarding bands not included in this question, The Who and The Rolling Stones celebrated their fifty-ninth and six-tieth anniversaries in 2022. Apologies if this question made you feel old, but in fairness it means you probably are.

3. C, B, D, A – Finland was named the world's happiest place to live for the fifth year in a row (Israel ninth, Germany fourteenth, United Kingdom seventeenth). The list is gen-erally accepted by most countries, except in North Korea where the list is topped every year by North Korea.

4. B, C, D, A – Of these four veterans, Sir Peter Bottomley is the current Father of the House, having served continu-ously since 1975 (Sheerman – 1979, Harman – 1982) and Sir Edward Leigh is one of five MPs who took their seats on 9 June 1983, including an exciting independent up-and-comer called Jeremy Corbyn.

5. D, B, A, C – The Big One at Blackpool (64.9 m) has been the UK's tallest rollercoaster since it opened in 1994 and pro-vides stunning panoramic views of hen parties throwing up outside kebab shops. In case you were wondering, Millennium measures 45.7 m, The Odyssey 50.9 m and Stealth 62.5 m.

6. B, D, C, A – Noble Yeats won, closely followed by Any Second Now and Delta Work. The Grand National's impeccable safety record was again highlighted, as Lostintranslation was the last horse to cross the line, placing fifteenth out of a field of forty horses.

7. C, B, A, D – Nigeria has the largest population in the list with 216 million. Russia is next with 145 million, then the UK with 68 million. Despite being the world's twelfth largest country, Greenland only has a population of 57,000, working out to 0.026 people per square kilometre, which is a lot less gruesome than it sounds.

8. D, C, A, B – The Australian Grand Prix attracted 128,894 fans (while the League Cup final drew in 85,512, Six Nations 81,621 and Super Bowl LVI 70,048), and they were treated to the holy grail of elite racing – Max Verstappen breaking down and walking solemnly back to the garage.

9. C, A, D, B – Victoria comes out on top here with sixty-three years served (George III – fifty-nine years, William IV – six years, Edward VIII – 327 days) but all of these pale in comparison to Louis XIV of France, who racked up seventy-two years (1643–1715).

10. C, A, B, D – *Coco* is by far the most recent, coming out in 2017 (*A Bug's Life* – 1998, *The Incredibles* – 2004, *WALL-E* – 2008) but if you really want your day ruining, when the original *Toy Story* came out John Major was still PM.

BACKBENCH MP OR CHARLES DICKENS CHARACTER?

Can you separate your Chuzzlewits from your Starmers, or the Fagins from the Rees-Moggs? Below are twenty names, but are you more likely to find them in Dickens or the Commons?

1. John Peerybingle
2. Diane Markleham
3. Flick Drummond
4. Tommy Sheppard
5. Wera Hobhouse
6. Fanny Squeers
7. Matthew Pennycook
8. Georgiana Podsnap
9. Bentley Drummle
10. Elizabeth Twist
11. Tim Linkinwater
12. Holly Mumby-Croft
13. Carla Lockhart
14. Marion Jeddler
15. Yvonne Fovargue
16. Robert Goodwill
17. William Guppy
18. Maggie Throup
19. Jon Trickett
20. Chevy Slyme

BACKBENCH MP OR CHARLES DICKENS CHARACTER? – ANSWERS

Backbench MPs

3. Flick Drummond (Meon Valley – Conservative)

4. Tommy Sheppard (Edinburgh East – Scottish National Party)

5. Wera Hobhouse (Bath – Liberal Democrats)

7. Matthew Pennycook (Greenwich and Woolwich – Labour)

10. Elizabeth Twist (Blaydon – Labour)

12. Holly Mumby-Croft (Scunthorpe – Conservative)

13. Carla Lockhart (Upper Bann – Democratic Unionist Party)

15. Yvonne Fovargue (Makerfield – Labour)

16. Robert Goodwill (Scarborough and Whitby – Conservative)

18. Maggie Throup (Erewash – Conservative)

19. Jon Trickett (Hemsworth – Labour)

Dickens Characters

1. John Peerybingle (*The Cricket on the Hearth* – 1845)

2. Diane Markleham (*David Copperfield* – 1850)

6. Fanny Squeers (*Nicholas Nickleby* – 1839)

8. Georgiana Podsnap (*Our Mutual Friend* – 1865)

9. Bentley Drummle (*Great Expectations* – 1861)

11. Tim Linkinwater (*Nicholas Nickleby* – 1839)

14. Marion Jeddler (*The Battle of Life* – 1846)

17. William Guppy (*Bleak House* – 1853)

20. Chevy Slyme (*Martin Chuzzlewit* – 1844)

CAPTAIN HINDSIGHT'S STARMY ARMY

How much can you remember about the Labour Party in 2022? Probably not very much, but thankfully the answers are multiple choice so you've got a fighting chance of getting at least one right. (Warning: some of the questions involve Keir Starmer, so don't attempt this round before driving or operating heavy machinery.)

1. Who was suspended from the Labour Party in 2022 after being branded a 'serial bully' by the Independent Expert Panel?

    A. John Prescott
    B. Melvyn Bragg
    C. Peter Mandelson
    D. John Bercow

2. A tweet by Labour's Manchester mayor Andy Burnham went viral early in the year when he highlighted the price of what?

    A. Food
    B. Rail fares
    C. Motorway toll roads
    D. Fuel

3. Keir Starmer said it would be 'very difficult' to allow Jeremy Corbyn to rejoin the party because of comments he'd made about what?

   A. The House of Lords

   B. Labour's climate stance

   C. NATO

   D. Trident

4. The Commons found itself embroiled in a sexism scandal when the *Mail on Sunday* accused Angela Rayner of distracting Boris Johnson using a tactic from which film?

   A. *When Harry Met Sally*

   B. *Basic Instinct*

   C. *Fatal Attraction*

   D. *Alien*

5. Pressure continued to ramp up over Keir Starmer's lockdown curry well into the summer, but can you remember which brand of beer he was drinking in the now-infamous photo?

   A. Peroni

   B. Newcastle Brown Ale

   C. San Miguel

   D. Hobgoblin

6. Durham Constabulary conducted the investigation into Keir Starmer's alleged breach of Covid rules, but who had they controversially not investigated for the same thing two years previously?

   A. John McDonnell
   B. Matt Hancock
   C. Jeremy Corbyn
   D. Dominic Cummings

7. Despite the government being made up of some of the most faceless politicians in history, Labour's front bench is even more anonymous. Which of the following MPs DIDN'T serve in Keir Starmer's shadow cabinet in 2022?

   A. John Healey
   B. Lucy Powell
   C. Peter Kyle
   D. Ron Dixon

8. In an interview with GB News in June, royal biographer Nigel Cawthorne claimed that former Labour leader Jeremy Corbyn could thwart what?

   A. The Jubilee Concert
   B. Charles's accession to the throne
   C. Plans for a new royal yacht
   D. Buckingham Palace refurbishments

9. During his statement to Parliament following the release of the full Sue Gray report, what did Boris Johnson call Keir Starmer?

   A. Beer Starmer

   B. Keir Korma

   C. Beer Korma

   D. Basil Balti

10. When Labour took control of Westminster City Council in May's local elections, which tourist attraction was said to be a key factor?

   A. Big Ben

   B. The London Eye

   C. Nelson's Column

   D. The Marble Arch Mound

Captain Hindsight's Starmy Army – Answers

1. D – The suspension came as bittersweet news to Bercow – who had defected to the party from the Conservatives in 2021 – as on the one hand he was being kicked out, but on the other, people were paying attention to him, and that's all that really matters.

2. B – It was about rail fares. Burnham pointed out that it's cheaper to fly to India or Jamaica and back than it is to get a return ticket from Manchester to London. Train companies vowed to offer better value for money after the tweet went viral, and many now offer a complimentary copy of *The Times* with tickets over £400.

3. C – Corbyn – a long-time critic of NATO – has consistently argued that the alliance is completely pointless and should fade away into obscurity, much like the example set by Momentum.

4. B – Rayner was accused of channelling Sharon Stone's character from *Basic Instinct* by crossing and uncrossing her legs to distract Boris Johnson, which is all rather unnecessary when the same can be achieved with a squeaky toy or by rattling some car keys.

5. C – He was drinking a bottle of San Miguel – a tad more exciting than his usual tipple of a single glass of room-temperature water. After being associated with Keir Starmer, bosses at San Miguel say they expect sales to recover by mid 2025.

6. D – It was Dominic Cummings, whose explanation for his actions was so utterly ridiculous that it beggars belief people treated everything he 'revealed' as gospel in 2022.

7. D – You'd be forgiven for having a stab in the dark on this one, but the answer is Ron Dixon. John Healey, Lucy Powell and Peter Kyle all featured in Keir Starmer's top team in 2022, whereas Ron Dixon was the bloke who ran the paper shop in Brookside.

8. B – It was claimed Corbyn could make things difficult for Charles due to his place on the Royal Accession Committee. Sticking an unpopular old bloke in the top job is always a risky move; just ask anyone who was a Labour MP between 2015 and 2020.

9. C – He called the Labour leader 'Beer Korma', although Starmer actually finds korma far too spicy.

10. D – Labour councillor Geoff Barraclough told the *Architects' Journal* that the Marble Arch Mound featured on all their leaflets as it shredded the council's reputation of being careful with taxpayers' money. The mound closed in January and was dismantled in May, despite offering stunning panoramic views of Oxford Street's 4,932 American candy shops.

WHAT'S IN A NAME?

The Washington Redskins, IMDb TV, and bizarrely, chicken Kievs all became known as something else in 2022 (Washington Commanders, Amazon Freevee and Chicken Kyivs respectively) but can you work out the following celebrities from their real names?

1. Stefani Joanne Angelina Germanotta
2. Maurice Joseph Micklewhite Jr
3. Mahershalalhashbaz Gilmore
4. Neta Lee Hershlag
5. Robyn Fenty
6. Eilleen Edwards
7. Aubrey Graham
8. Ella Marija Lani Yelich-O'Connor
9. Mark Sinclair Vincent
10. Katheryn Hudson
11. Nicolas Kim Coppola
12. Shelton Jackson Lee
13. Caryn Elaine Johnson
14. Abel Makkonen Tesfaye
15. Alecia Beth Moore
16. Krishna Pandit Bhanji
17. Peter Gene Hernandez
18. Paul David Hewson
19. Melissa Jefferson
20. Eric Marlon Bishop

WHAT'S IN A NAME? – ANSWERS

1. American singer-turned-actor **Lady Gaga**

2. Star of *The Italian Job* and *Zulu* **Sir Michael Caine**

3. Two-time Oscar winner **Mahershala Ali**

4. *Black Swan* and *Star Wars* actress **Natalie Portman**

5. Barbadian singer and fashion icon **Rihanna**

6. Hard-to-impress country star **Shania Twain**

7. Canadian rapper **Drake**

8. Charismatic New Zealand singer-songwriter **Lorde**

9. American tough guy actor **Vin Diesel**

10. 'Teenage Dream' singer **Katy Perry**

11. Dulcet-toned star of *Con Air* and *National Treasure* **Nicolas Cage**

12. Legendary American film director **Spike Lee**

13. Actress and everyone's favourite singing nun **Whoopi Goldberg**

14. Canadian singer and producer **The Weeknd**

15. Pop punk queen **P!nk**

16. Oscar-winning *Gandhi* actor **Sir Ben Kingsley**

17. Diminutive 'Uptown Funk' singer **Bruno Mars**

18. Universally loved U2 frontman **Bono**

19. 'Good as Hell' singer and body-positivity activist **Lizzo**

20. Multi-talented star of *Ray* and *Collateral* **Jamie Foxx**

FAKE NEWS!!!

Can you tell the real 2022 headlines from the ones that are completely made up? This might have been easy when a year's worth of news didn't happen on a daily basis, but we haven't been that lucky since about 1998.

1. Sir Rod Stewart fills potholes in Celtic gear outside home as his 'Ferrari can't drive through'.
2. Matt Hancock to run Essex Half Marathon dressed as a fair-trade banana.
3. French Bulldog dressed as David Bowie stars at Oscar-themed dog pageant.
4. Giant New Zealand potato is not in fact a potato, Guinness World Records rules.
5. Big Ben's scaffolding to be partially rebuilt to allow builder to retrieve toolbox.
6. Flamingo that fled US zoo 17 years ago spotted alive and well after 700-mile trip.
7. Man 'no longer friends' with pal who bought him 'traumatising' £11 fry-up.
8. As the cost-of-living crisis hits, Rishi Sunak weighs up sunny Easter break at Center Parcs.
9. Donald Trump releases official statement claiming he hit an eagle during recent round of golf.
10. 'My Tinder date broke into my home and filled my shoes with spaghetti.'

FAKE NEWS!!! – ANSWERS

1. Real – Essex Highways issued a warning after Sir Rod took the roadworks into his own hands, although he was applauded by the DWP for proving that seventy-seven-year-olds are still capable of manual labour (BBC – 13 March).

2. Fake news! – Hancock did however complete the 2021 London Marathon, and registered a four-minute mile after spotting his wife near the start line.

3. Fake news! – A bulldog dressed as David Bowie would be ridiculous. It was actually a Pomeranian dressed as Sir Elton John.

4. Real – Officials ruled that the 'potato' was in fact a gourd tuber. The gourd's disappointed owner said he discovered it last August after finding it with a hoe, although what he does in his own time is his business (*Guardian* – 16 March).

5. Fake news! – Big Ben's scaffolding did finally come down in 2022, however, and after five years and £80 million, it looked pretty much the same as before. Could have just asked Fathers 4 Justice to give it a quick dusting next time they were going up there.

6. Real – The flamingo, known as Pink Floyd, was spotted in Texas after going missing from a Kansas zoo in 2005. Zookeepers say they tried to convince it to come back but unfortunately it put its foot down (*Guardian* – 1 April).

7. Real – The breakfast, bought in Hampshire, had all the staples of a classic fry-up, as well as grapefruit, pomegranate and a side garnish of rocket. Also worth mentioning that if a fry-up costs £11 and doesn't block at least one artery then what's the point? (*Mirror* – 20 March)

8. Fake news! – The last thing Sunak would do when people are struggling is pack his bags and go to Center Parcs. He wouldn't be seen dead there – it was actually his luxury flat in California.

9. Fake news! – Trump did release an official statement, but rather than an eagle he claimed to have hit a hole in one. It definitely happened of course, but is well short of the eleven holes-in-one that North Korean leader Kim Jong-il claimed to have hit during his first ever round of golf.

10. Real – A woman in Ipswich returned home to find her shoes filled with pasta. Police say such offences are rare, and are limited to a fusilli individuals (*Daily Star* – 31 March).

IT'S A ROYAL COCK-UP – ROUND 1

Before the Queen's sad death in September, the royal family attempted to cheer everyone up in the best possible way – four days of getting smashed in the name of Her Majesty's seventy years on the throne. And though it's possible you don't remember much from that particular weekend, see how you fare with these questions instead.

1. Prince Andrew cleared his name by agreeing an out-of-court settlement with a woman he'd apparently never met (as you do) but during his infamous *Newsnight* interview back in November 2019, where did he claim to be on the night he didn't meet her?

    A. Nando's
    B. At the cinema
    C. Scotland
    D. Pizza Express

2. In March it was revealed that the Queen would never again do what?

    A. Travel abroad
    B. Live in London
    C. Carry out royal duties
    D. Support Prince Andrew

3. As the media desperately tried to keep Meghan Markle's purported feud with the royals going, bombshell allegations claimed she once argued with the Queen over what?

   A. Eggs
   B. Cheese
   C. Wine
   D. Chicken nuggets

4. The Duke and Duchess of Cambridge's trip to the Caribbean was marred by protests and calls to cut ties with the monarchy, but which of the following countries did they NOT visit?

   A. Jamaica
   B. Belize
   C. The Bahamas
   D. Dominican Republic

5. Not to be outdone by his brother, Prince Harry's popularity also continued to nosedive in 2022. Which unusual sporting event was the Duke of Sussex spotted at in early March?

   A. Lawnmower racing
   B. Texas rodeo
   C. Professional beer pong
   D. Wife-carrying championships

6. During the (then) Duke and Duchess of Cornwall's spring visit to East Belfast, a royal fan managed to grab Prince Charles' attention using a fake what?

    A. Bunch of flowers

    B. Parrot

    C. Fabergé egg

    D. Baby

7. During an official engagement in April, Camilla revealed that the royals had voted for which *Strictly Come Dancing* contestant?

    A. AJ Odudu

    B. Adam Peaty

    C. Rose Ayling-Ellis

    D. Tom Fletcher

8. A few days later, Prince Andrew dipped his toe back into the world of social media but immediately deleted a seven-hundred-word post about what?

    A. Prince Harry

    B. Horse-riding

    C. The Falklands War

    D. His favourite pizza toppings

9. But before the post was deleted entirely, eagle-eyed observers noticed that it was edited. Why?

   A. The attached photo had been altered
   B. He had misspelled the Queen's name
   C. It included an offensive hashtag
   D. It included his old royal titles

10. In April, Tory MPs lobbied No. 10 to allow the royal family to use what?

    A. Boris Johnson's plane
    B. A seized Russian super-yacht
    C. Gold bullion to pay off debt
    D. The hard shoulder of the M25

It's a Royal Cock-up – Round 1 Answers

1. D – It was of course the Woking branch of Pizza Express, although he presumably went in full camo, as nobody can remember seeing him.

2. B – It was confirmed that the Queen was to make Windsor Castle her permanent residence and would never again live in London. It had been long rumoured that she was planning on moving house after staff at her local Morrison's confirmed she'd been in a few times looking for cardboard boxes.

3. A – The row apparently took place during a tasting session ahead of Meghan's wedding to Prince Harry, when the Queen is said to have reprimanded her over claiming to taste eggs in an 'egg-free' dish. Thankfully *Jeremy Kyle* is no longer on the air or this could have really spiralled out of control.

4. D – The ill-advised trip was a catastrophic failure from start to finish and caused major headaches, for both the royal family and *Daily Mail* journalists desperately working out how to pin it on Meghan Markle.

5. B – Harry was spotted amongst the crowd in early March, possibly weighing up a new career as a rodeo clown (not to be confused with Prince Andrew, who is a regular one).

6. A – The woman managed to grab Charles's attention with a bouquet of fake flowers which, much to the disappointment of onlookers, wasn't rigged up to squirt water.

7. C – During a visit to the set of *EastEnders*, Camilla said she couldn't believe how Ayling-Ellis managed to perform despite not being able to hear the music. It also marked a rare occasion where a royal visit involved actual deafness, without being preceded by 'tone'.

8. C – The post, on Sarah Ferguson's Instagram account, said that he returned from the Falklands 'a changed man' – presumably the bit where it made his sweat glands fall off.

9. D – The post initially said it was written by 'HRH The Duke of York' before the HRH was swiftly removed. Although Andrew lost his royal and military titles in January, the British public has since invented hundreds of unofficial new ones, none of which can be repeated here.

10. B – To be fair this is quite a good idea, as there would be nothing more horrifying to a yacht-owning oligarch than the thought of Charles and Camilla skinny-dipping off the side of it.

FEEL OLD YET?

The following things/people all reached significant milestones in 2022, but can you work them out from the clues below? (Bonus depressing facts: 2022 is closer to 2050 than 1990, and there are people now driving in the UK who weren't born when Facebook was launched.)

1. Cult British album that turned twenty-five on 21 May. Includes songs 'No Surprises', 'Karma Police' and 'Exit Music (For a Film)'. In 2015 it was archived in the US Library of Congress due to its 'cultural significance'.

2. Book that was released twenty-five years ago, on 26 June 1997. It has sold more than 120 million copies, been translated into more than seventy languages and was adapted into one of the most successful film franchises of all time. Not bad for a debut novel.

3. Broadway musical that celebrated its fortieth anniversary on 9 May. Raul Julia, Jonathan Pryce and Antonio Banderas have all played the leading role, and in 2009 it was adapted into a film starring Daniel Day-Lewis, Nicole Kidman and Dame Judi Dench.

4. This British soap opera – set in the Yorkshire Dales – turned fifty on 16 October. It underwent a name change in 1989 and achieved its highest-ever viewing figures in 1993 with an ambitious storyline about an air disaster.

5. British hip-hop album that was released twenty years ago on 25 March 2002, after being recorded on a shoestring budget in a rented room in Brixton. Tracks include 'Weak Become Heroes', 'Turn the Page' and 'Let's Push Things Forward'.

6. Legendary composer who turned ninety on 8 February. Responsible for the film scores of *Jaws*, *Home Alone* and *Jurassic Park* to name a few. Winner of five Academy Awards, four Golden Globes and twenty-five Grammys.

7. This British TV personality celebrated her eightieth birthday on 25 March. One of the UK's leading authorities on dirty houses, she appeared in *Celebrity Big Brother* and *I'm a Celebrity . . . Get Me Out of Here!* where she finished second to Gino D'Acampo.

8. This album, from one of the UK's most treasured artists, was released fifty years ago on 16 June 1972. Sung from the perspective of an alien rockstar sent to Earth, it includes tracks 'Moonage Daydream', 'Suffragette City' and 'Rock 'n' Roll Suicide'.

9. This sequel to one of the most beloved Christmas films of all time turned thirty in 2022, and featured appearances from Rob Schneider, Brenda Fricker and bizarrely, Donald Trump.

10. And because you'll now likely be feeling a hundred years old, name the cult horror film that celebrated its hundredth birthday in 2022. Starring Max Schreck in the lead role, the film was loosely based on Bram Stoker's *Dracula*.

FEEL OLD YET? – ANSWERS

1. *OK Computer* – Radiohead

2. *Harry Potter and the Philosopher's Stone* – J.K. Rowling

3. *Nine*

4. *Emmerdale* (previously *Emmerdale Farm*)

5. *Original Pirate Material* – The Streets

6. John Williams

7. Kim Woodburn

8. *The Rise and Fall of Ziggy Stardust and the Spiders from Mars* – David Bowie

9. *Home Alone 2: Lost in New York*

10. *Nosferatu: Eine Symphonie des Grauens*

Spot the Fake Channel 4 Show

One of the government's (many) unpopular decisions in 2022 came when then Culture Secretary Nadine Dorries announced plans to privatise Channel 4. As well as long-running favourites like *Countdown* and *Gogglebox*, the channel has never shied away from the weird and wonderful. Can you work out which of the following are real Channel 4 shows and which ones are completely made up?

1. **The Man with a Penis on His Arm** – Does what it says on the tin really. There's a bloke, and on his arm is a penis.

2. **Tree of the Year with Ardal O'Hanlon** – Tree-of-the-year competitions have been commonplace in Europe for years, but this one features Dougal from *Father Ted* for some reason.

3. **Mother-in-Lord** – Six born-again priests must reconcile with their ex-partners' mums after leaving their daughters for a life in the church.

4. **I Married an Octopus** – Documentary about a forty-six-year-old woman from Northampton who moved to Cyprus and attempted to marry an octopus called Lancelot.

5. **London's Sexiest Landlords** – This four-part series follows some of the capital's dreamiest property moguls as they explain why vital plumbing work can wait until next August.

6. **Drugs Live** – People take drugs, and ... well, that's about it really.

7. **America's Biggest Mushrooms with Phil Tufnell** – The former England spin-bowler visits several of North America's largest mushrooms, including a 3,000-square-foot fungus beneath Yellowstone National Park.

8. **Sex Box** – Couples go into a giant box and have sex inside it. They then emerge from the giant box and tell the audience about ... well, the sex they just had in the giant box.

9. **Game of Clones** – Reality show where people describe their perfect partner, then move in with eight near-identical matches who fit the description.

10. **Carjackers** – People arrange to have cars belonging to their friends and family stolen in order to give them shocking makeovers.

11. **Help, I'm Dead!** – Sixty-four-year-old Brenda from Doncaster believes she died in her sleep in 1992, but can still communicate with people (and TV cameras) for some reason.

12. **The Boy Who Can Talk to Cheese** – Steve Jones spends a week with eleven-year-old Maxwell from Denver, Colorado who claims he can communicate with cheese.

13. **The British Tribe Next Door** – Scarlett Moffatt and her family move into an exact replica of their terraced house, which has been painstakingly built in the middle of a remote African village.

14. **Are We There Yet?** Take four mates, put them in a car and see how long it takes for the passengers to realise they're just going round in circles. The driver wins £10 for every mile travelled without anyone realising.

15. **Meat the Family** – A family of meat-eaters has to look after an animal for a week, and then decide whether they want to A: eat their new pet or B: send them to a sanctuary and never eat meat again.

Spot the Fake Channel 4 Show – Answers

Real

1. The Man with a Penis on His Arm

2. Tree of the Year with Ardal O'Hanlon

6. Drugs Live

8. Sex Box

9. Game of Clones

10. Carjackers

13. The British Tribe Next Door

15. Meat the Family

Fake

3. Mother-in-Lord

4. I Married an Octopus

5. London's Sexiest Landlords

7. America's Biggest Mushrooms with Phil Tufnell

11. Help, I'm Dead!

12. The Boy Who Can Talk to Cheese

14. Are We There Yet?

ACROSS THE POND

As unhinged as things seemed in the UK in 2022, you can always count on the US to make us seem comparatively ... well, hinged. Here are ten questions about America.

1. In May, 192 Republicans voted against a bill for $28 million to tackle a national shortage of what?

    A. Insulin
    B. Birth control pills
    C. Formula milk
    D. Wheat

2. During a speech in Texas, America's second most gaffe-prone president, George W. Bush, was left red-faced after accidentally condemning what?

    A. The Republican Party
    B. One of his dad's policies
    C. A local war veterans' charity
    D. The invasion of Iraq

3. What was unusual when Oregon resident Elizabeth Johnson Jr was exonerated by lawmakers in May?

    A. She died in the seventeenth century

    B. She pleaded guilty to all charges

    C. One of the witnesses was a dog

    D. Hulk Hogan was her lawyer

4. By far one of the most inflammatory news stories of the year came when the US Supreme Court overturned 1973's landmark Roe vs Wade abortion ruling. Following the decision, what did Pope Francis compare terminations to?

    A. A terrorist attack

    B. Hiring a hitman

    C. Slapping God in the face

    D. Blowing up a hospital

5. After Donald Trump's Mar-a-Lago beach resort was raided by the FBI in August, the unsealed warrant listed several boxes of top-secret documents, as well as information about the president of which country?

    A. Brazil

    B. Canada

    C. France

    D. Turkey

6. One sad inevitability of the US coming out of lockdown was the return of preventable gun violence. After three mass shootings in four weeks, House Minority Leader Kevin McCarthy said that schools should use Covid funds to do what?

    A. Hold active shooter training
    B. Install alarms
    C. Fortify classrooms
    D. Get rid of doors

7. Donald Trump also weighed in on the gun issue, saying that funding safe schools should take priority over what?

    A. Trade talks with the UK
    B. Supporting LGBTQ+ issues
    C. Sending aid to Ukraine
    D. Investigating his tax returns

8. In late May a video of Kendall Jenner went viral after she attempted which near-impossible task?

    A. Folding a bedsheet
    B. Boiling an egg
    C. Chopping a cucumber
    D. Using a lawnmower

9. Which social media platform was fined $150 million in the US for selling users' data?

   A. Twitter
   B. Facebook
   C. TikTok
   D. Instagram

10. After allegedly being told not to say 'gay' during a graduation speech in his increasingly conservative (backwards) home state of Florida, what did high school student Zander Moricz replace the word with to ensure the mic wasn't cut off?

   A. 'Oranges'
   B. 'Refrigerator'
   C. 'Curly hair'
   D. 'Love'

ACROSS THE POND – ANSWERS

1. C – It was to address a shortage of baby formula milk. Republicans spent much of the year claiming to be the party of 'pro-life', but only until birth of course, at which point people can starve, or if they're lucky, grow old enough to be shot at school.

2. D – Bush accidentally criticised the invasion of Iraq, saying 'The result is an absence of checks and balances in Russia, and the decision of one man to launch a wholly unjustified and brutal invasion of Iraq.' But in fairness, Freudian slips are much more likely when your surname is Bush.

3. A – Johnson Jr was the final Salem 'witch' to be exonerated, having been sentenced to death in 1693, although the Supreme Court hasn't ruled out bringing back witch trials when it moves on from reproductive rights.

4. B – Pope Francis likened abortions to hiring a hitman, a stance that he's reiterated many times over the years. The Catholic Church does – after all – have a long history of maintaining the safety and wellbeing of young children.

5. C – The warrant listed 'info re: President of France'. (It didn't detail which president, but it's hard to imagine Trump brushing up on Patrice de MacMahon, Duke of Magenta.) The raid – which led to Trump being investigated for espionage, of all things – included a search of his personal safe, which agents were able to crack after finding '0000' written on the back of his hand.

6. D – The root of the problem is doors apparently. Republicans claimed that reducing the number of doors in schools would put shooters off, as they'd almost definitely give up and go home if faced with walking an extra twenty feet to a different entrance.

7. C – Trump urged lawmakers to focus on making schools safe before sending military aid to Ukraine. Bit of an unfair comparison really, as the American school system is far more dangerous than Ukraine.

8. C – Kendall Jenner hit the headlines after struggling to cut a cucumber on an episode of *Keeping Up with the Kardashians*. FYI, be careful when typing 'Kendall Jenner cucumber' into Google, as it turns out there's some very disturbing fan art out there.

9. A – Twitter was fined for selling data to third-party advertisers, although it's not clear how much market research you can really gather from Russian bots and racial slurs.

10. C – Video of the speech went viral as Zander talked about his curly hair, how difficult it was to accept his curly hair and how his friends helped him come to terms with his curly hair in the humid state of Florida. Republicans responded by immediately banning children from having hair.

ALL MIXED UP – ROUND 1

In May, Anne Robinson announced she was quitting as *Countdown* host, which is handy as we needed a segue into a round of '*Countdown* Conundrums' – that's anagrams to you and me. Can you work out the following mixed-up people/things that made headlines in 2022?

1. GAL HIJACKERS – English footballer. Picked up a Premier League winners' medal.
2. CANOPY LINES – Current US politician. Donald Trump isn't a fan.
3. MOUSE BAIT – Professional dancer. Left *Strictly* in 2022 and toured the UK.
4. HUMANIST TWEED – British football club. Had a decent run in Europe.
5. SALTY SHERRY – Ex-boyband member. Released a number-one album in May.
6. DINNER GEL – Critically acclaimed video game released in February. Hard as nails.
7. ANTHEM TAB – 2022 superhero reboot. Took £13.5 million in the UK on opening weekend.
8. AGONISING DREAM – US stadium rockers. Played a huge show in Milton Keynes.
9. DANDELION SEEDS – Current member of the shadow cabinet and MP for Oxford East.
10. AABSEILING – Irish comedian. Appeared in the New Year's Day *Doctor Who* special.

11. ARSING STRENGTH – Popular Netflix show. Its penultimate season aired in 2022.

12. CRAPPIER RAP – Journalist with an impressive collection of party videos. Probably not on Boris Johnson's Christmas card list.

13. CRINKLED KARMA – US Rapper. Released one of the biggest albums of the year.

14. DRUG INTERN – Animated film added to Disney+ in March. Made headlines for highlighting 'taboo' topics.

15. CLEO JETTY – Birmingham comedian. Spent time holidaying with other comedians on Channel 4.

16. FANTASISTS POSTIES – Tennis player. Reached the semis of the Australian Open.

17. HOOTING MNK – 2022 Disney series. Star Wars actor trying out another franchise.

18. BEVVY EDEN GLEE – Life peer. Came under intense media scrutiny in early 2022.

19. HIP CANDLE – 2022 reboot of a popular 90s cartoon. Stars Eric Bana and Will Arnett.

20. ABSENT LEVITATES – F1 driver. A former world champion who has fallen down the pecking order in recent years, driving for Aston Martin in 2022.

21. ASIAN RODS – Played her first UK gig since 2007 at the Queen's Jubilee Concert.

22. ACHILLES COMING – Scottish long-distance runner. Won two medals at the 2022 Commonwealth Games in Birmingham.

23. BALMY PEA PINK – French footballer. Not very popular in Madrid after rejecting a move to Real in May.

24. HOLISM MADONNA – Former *Big Brother* housemate. Now a TV presenter; appeared alongside Dermot O'Leary on daytime TV in 2022.

25. CAVING GOTH VENN – Painter. Was immortalised as an official Lego set in May.

ALL MIXED UP – ROUND 1 ANSWERS

1. Jack Grealish

2. Nancy Pelosi

3. Oti Mabuse

4. West Ham United

5. Harry Styles

6. Elden Ring

7. *The Batman*

8. Imagine Dragons

9. Anneliese Dodds

10. Aisling Bea

11. *Stranger Things*

12. Pippa Crerar

13. Kendrick Lamar

14. *Turning Red*

15. Joe Lycett

16. Stefanos Tsitsipas

17. *Moon Knight*

18. Evgeny Lebedev

19. *Chip 'n' Dale*

20. Sebastian Vettel

21. Diana Ross

22. Eilish McColgan

23. Kylian Mbappé

24. Alison Hammond

25. Vincent van Gogh

WHO SAID IT? JACOB REES-MOGG OR SAMUEL PEPYS

One's a seventeenth-century symbol of high society; the other is Samuel Pepys, but who said what?

1. 'God made man in his own image. He made man and he made woman. He made both of them. I think God making us in his own image is quite good enough for me.'
2. 'Never since I was a man in the world was I ever so great a stranger to public affairs as now I am.'
3. 'This being a very pleasant life that we now lead, and have long done; the Lord be blessed and make us thankful.'
4. 'All they care about is cake and animals.'
5. 'The strict disciplining of a child not yet a fortnight old would be unreasonable by any standards. All I can say is that I am glad not to be an infant in his household.'
6. 'Great talk among people how some of the fanatics do say that the end of the world is at hand.'
7. 'As for Magdalen College, it is not exactly 1687–88. It is a few pimply adolescents getting excited and taking down a picture of Her Majesty.'
8. 'I did then desire to know what was the great matter that grounded his desire for the Chancellor's removal.'
9. 'For I eat my own lamb, my own chicken and ham. I shear my own fleece and I wear it.'
10. 'Strange, to see what delight we married people have to see these poor fools decoyed into our condition.'

Who Said It? Jacob Rees-Mogg or Samuel Pepys – Answers

1. Jacob Rees-Mogg

LBC – 4 April 2022

2. Samuel Pepys

Diary entry – 10 August 1660. Robert Latham, *The Illustrated Pepys* (London: Bell & Hyman Limited, 1978), p. 24

3. Samuel Pepys

Diary entry – 20 May 1662. Latham, *The Illustrated Pepys*, p. 39

4. Jacob Rees-Mogg

House of Commons – 27 January 2022

5. Jacob Rees-Mogg

House of Commons – 17 July 2017

6. Samuel Pepys

Diary entry – 25 November 1662. Latham, *The Illustrated Pepys*, p. 45

7. Jacob Rees-Mogg

House of Commons – 10 June 2021

8. Samuel Pepys

> Diary entry – 2 September 1667. Latham, *The Illustrated Pepys*, p. 155

9. Jacob Rees–Mogg

> House of Commons – 12 November 2010

10. Samuel Pepys

> Diary entry – 25 December 1665. Latham, *The Illustrated Pepys*, p. 96

As fuel costs spiralled out of control, Jacob Rees-Mogg
was praised by environmentalists after the national
rollout of his alternative to the Boris Bike:

WHAT HAPPENED NEXT?

If 2022 taught us anything, it was to expect the unexpected. Can you remember what came next in these ten stories?

1. During a raucous PMQs in early January, when MP after MP lined up to call for Boris Johnson's resignation over Downing Street parties during lockdown, Tory backbencher Alberto Costa cleared his throat, stood up and asked a question about which pressing issue?

    A. Bins
    B. Bicycles
    C. Washing machines
    D. Badgers

2. Early in the year a clip of a monkey at Chester Zoo went viral after it scaled a twenty-foot pole and did what?

    A. Flung poo at onlookers
    B. Raised its middle finger
    C. Killed a seagull
    D. Escaped from the enclosure

3. Ohio news reporter Myles Harris made headlines when what happened in the middle of a live TV broadcast?

    A. A bird landed on his head

    B. He fell down a manhole

    C. A carrier bag hit him in the face

    D. He was embarrassed by his mum

4. During Ed Sheeran's plagiarism court case, one of his songs was played from co-writer Steven McCutcheon's laptop, causing Sheeran to look at his lawyers in confusion. What was wrong?

    A. A private conversation could be heard

    B. It played a never-before-heard song

    C. It wasn't one of his songs

    D. The laptop was knocked onto the floor

5. During Everton's home game against Newcastle in the Premier League, a protestor ran onto the pitch and did what?

    A. Popped the ball

    B. Tied themself to the goal

    C. Showed the referee a red card

    D. Stole the mascot's head

6. During the dreaded interviews section of the TV show *The Apprentice*, no-nonsense Mike Souter asked contestant Kathryn Burn whether she'd registered the domain name for her pyjama company. She had not. What did Mike then reveal?

    A. It invalidated her business plan
    B. It was already in use by a rival company
    C. That he'd like to invest in her
    D. He had purchased the domain name

7. In early March, Indian news anchor Rahul Shivshankar spent almost two minutes passionately berating US foreign policy expert Daniel McAdams while Ukrainian journalist Bohdan Nahaylo looked on. What became apparent when McAdams finally got a chance to speak?

    A. They'd all been on mute
    B. He'd been shouting at the wrong person
    C. It was offensive in German
    D. Nahaylo had fallen asleep

8. During the Supreme Court hearing for Biden nominee Ketanji Brown Jackson, Texas Senator Ted Cruz went off on one of his trademark performative outbursts. Moments later, people sitting behind him spotted him doing what?

    A. Looking at porn
    B. Eating a boiled egg
    C. Searching for himself on Twitter
    D. Making rude gestures

9. After P&O Ferries laid off eight hundred workers in order to replace them with cheaper agency staff, Dover MP Natalie Elphicke confidently marched back to her constituency to offer support, but was roundly heckled by protestors because of what?

    A. Taking too long to respond
    B. Her choice of clothing
    C. Leaving after a photo op
    D. Her voting record

10. At the 2022 Oscars ceremony, comedian Chris Rock was presenting the award for best documentary when what happened?

    A. He fell off the stage
    B. He was drowned out by boos
    C. His mic was cut
    D. He was slapped in the face

WHAT HAPPENED NEXT? – ANSWERS

1. C – The MP for South Leicestershire heroically dared to ask the question on everyone's lips and forced Boris Johnson to reveal where he stood on the issue of microplastic filters fitted to new washing machines.

2. C – Visitors watched in horror as the monkey grabbed a seagull, savagely beat it to death and ate it. Horrifying, but not horrifying enough to stop people adding the opening theme from *The Lion King* and uploading it to TikTok.

3. D – Harris was left red-faced after his mum Sandi pulled up in a car while he was reporting live and shouted 'hi baby!' through the window. Thankfully she was moved along before she could reach for the school photos and swimming certificates.

4. B – The track was unreleased, which some would argue is the best kind of Ed Sheeran song.

5. B – After a protestor tied himself to the goal, the situation became even more farcical when a member of Everton's backroom staff ran onto the pitch with an enormous pair of bolt cutters to cut through a single plastic cable tie. To be fair, tying yourself to the goal at Everton is one of the safer places to protest, as you're extremely unlikely to be hit by anything.

6. D – Souter hadn't just bought one domain name, but also any domain names that were remotely similar. He did however gift one of them back to contestant Burn and she went through to the final, which she promptly lost, so the whole thing was a huge waste of time really.

7. B – Shivshankar had been shouting at the wrong person after a technical mix-up transposed his guests' names onscreen. To be fair, it was impossible for him to have known the person he was talking to wasn't McAdams, as his only clue was the American guy trying to interject with a thick Ukrainian accent.

8. C – Cruz was left red-faced after being snapped searching for mentions of his name on Twitter, which for Ted can surely never be a good thing. You'd be forgiven for picking A here though, as his official account famously liked a porn tweet on the anniversary of 9/11 in 2017.

9. D – Elphicke arrived in Dover to march in solidarity with sacked staff, but was politely reminded by protestors that she voted against a bill to stop companies doing precisely what P&O did. She did provide a bit of light relief however by joining in on a chant of 'shame on you' before realising it was directed at her.

10. D – After taking exception to a joke about his wife, Will Smith marched on stage and struck Rock with an open-handed slap, proving once and for all that paper does indeed defeat Rock.

WHOSE LIFE IS IT ANYWAY?

The following autobiographies were all published in 2022, but can you guess who wrote them from just the title?

1. *Friends, Lovers, and the Big Terrible Thing: A Memoir*
    A. Matthew Perry
    B. Lisa Kudrow
    C. Matt LeBlanc
    D. Courtney Cox

2. *The People's Game: A View from a Front Seat in Football*
    A. Martin Tyler
    B. John Motson
    C. Gary Neville
    D. Guy Mowbray

3. *Out of the Corner: A Memoir*
    A. Molly Ringwald
    B. Michelle Pfeiffer
    C. Heather Locklear
    D. Jennifer Grey

4. *Tough: My Journey to True Power*

   A. Vin Diesel
   B. Danny Trejo
   C. Ron Perlman
   D. Terry Crews

5. *Calling the Shots: My Autobiography*

   A. Clare Balding
   B. Sue Barker
   C. Gabby Logan
   D. Ant McPartlin

6. *A Different Stage*

   A. Gary Barlow
   B. Ronan Keating
   C. Duncan James
   D. Max George

7. *Ten: The Decade that Changed my Future*

   A. Joey Essex
   B. Scarlett Moffatt
   C. Rylan Clark
   D. Gemma Collins

8. *Finding My Own Rhythm: My Story*

    A. Craig Revel Horwood

    B. Motsi Mabuse

    C. Bruno Tonioli

    D. Darcey Bussell

9. *How (Not) to be Strong*

    A. Jessica Ennis-Hill

    B. Laura Kenny

    C. Paula Radcliffe

    D. Alex Scott

10. *Keep Talking: A Broadcasting Life*

    A. David Dimbleby

    B. Michael Parkinson

    C. Fiona Bruce

    D. Jonathan Ross

WHOSE LIFE IS IT ANYWAY?

1. A – Matthew Perry

2. C – Gary Neville

3. D – Jennifer Grey

4. D – Terry Crews

5. B – Sue Barker

6. A – Gary Barlow

7. C – Rylan Clark

8. B – Motsi Mabuse

9. D – Alex Scott

10. A – David Dimbleby

WHOSE BALD BONCE IS THIS?

Can you name these six follicly challenged men who made headlines in 2022? To make things easier we've included the eyebrows, so it doesn't just look like a box of eggs.

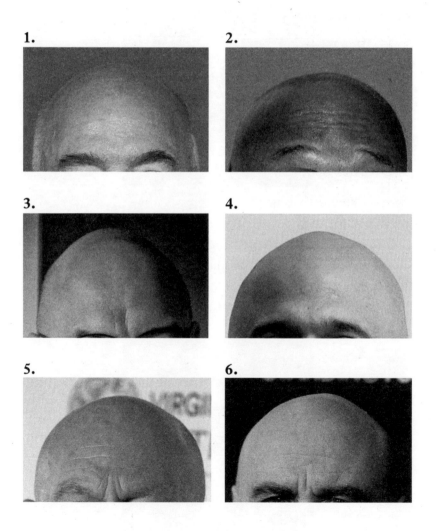

1.

2.

3.

4.

5.

6.

WHOSE BALD BONCE IS THIS? – ANSWERS

1. Jeff Bezos – In a year otherwise devoid of feel-good moments, the Amazon founder briefly cheered everyone up by losing $21 billion in a single day when the company's shares nosedived in April.

2. Samuel L. Jackson – Arguably the coolest slaphead on the list (and possibly the planet), the actor received an honorary Oscar for lifetime achievement at the Academy of Motion Picture Arts and Sciences' Governors Awards.

3. Gregg Wallace – A tricky one, this, as the excitable *Inside the Factory* presenter is normally seen wearing a superfluous hairnet. He nevertheless stunned viewers in 2022 with his new physique after hitting the weights and shedding four stone. Or as he would say, 'FOUR STONE!!!'

4. Sajid Javid – The ministerial journeyman was one of many MPs whose finances came under scrutiny in 2022 when it was revealed he'd used an offshore trust while working at the Treasury under George Osborne. Full of surprises, Tory MPs, aren't they?

5. Ross Kemp – The master of pointless documentaries struck again in 2022 with the sprawling epic *Searching for Michael Jackson's Zoo with Ross Kemp*. (Spoiler – he found the zoo.)

6. John Travolta – Early in 2022, Travolta swapped Tinseltown for Norfolk while shooting a short film, with sightings of the *Grease* legend being reported across the county, including at Fakenham Morrisons, where he autographed a fan's pack of sausage rolls.

THE IDIOT BOX

Heading into the year it didn't seem likely that we'd be watching as much TV as we did in 2020 or 2021, but we did anyway because lockdown(s) have rendered many of us completely immobile. Here are ten questions about television in 2022.

1. What was unusual about seventy-four-year-old Ken Smith's appearance at the Glasgow Film Festival in March?

    A. He arrived on a hovercraft
    B. He was reunited with his long-lost son
    C. He'd been living as a hermit since the 1980s
    D. He was wearing a full suit of armour

2. Martin Freeman was praised for his portrayal of police response officer Chris Carson in *The Responder*, but which aspect of the show did Sir Alan Sugar complain about on Twitter?

    A. The acting
    B. Its portrayal of Liverpool
    C. The lighting
    D. The accents

3. *The Masked Singer* was won by Natalie Imbruglia dressed as a giant panda (because of course it was) but over on the US version, the reveal of which contestant caused two judges to storm off stage in disgust?

    A. Alex Jones

    B. Marilyn Manson

    C. Rudy Giuliani

    D. Piers Morgan

4. In May it was confirmed that Jodie Whittaker would hand the keys of the Tardis to *Sex Education* star Ncuti Gatwa. Which of the following actors has not played the Doctor?

    A. Paul McGann

    B. Patrick Troughton

    C. Richard Hurndall

    D. Richard Briers

5. Ahead of the release of the second season of Netflix period drama *Bridgerton*, which unusual prop was revealed as the secret behind the show's numerous sex scenes?

    A. A netball

    B. A teddy bear

    C. A pin cushion

    D. A vacuum cleaner

6. While standing in for Richard Madeley on *Good Morning Britain*, Ed Balls was presented with a 'luxury merchandise package' from which TV show after admitting he's a huge fan?

    A. *Love Island*

    B. *Loose Women*

    C. *Dancing on Ice*

    D. *Ru Paul's Drag Race*

7. When *Minder* actor Dennis Waterman died in May, who did Kay Burley accidentally pay tribute to on Twitter?

    A. Rick Wakeman

    B. Gary Numan

    C. Pete Waterman

    D. Steve McManaman

8. On 29 June which programme – described by the *Guardian* as 'the most puerile show on TV' – was cancelled after fourteen years?

    A. *Mrs Brown's Boys*

    B. *Russell Howard's Good News*

    C. *Celebrity Juice*

    D. *Naked Attraction*

9. Why was *Good Morning Britain* presenter Alex Beresford criticised by co-hosts Adil Ray and Charlotte Hawkins while reporting from Buckingham Palace during the Queen's Platinum Jubilee?

   A. He sneezed into his hand
   B. His head was blocking the royals
   C. He wasn't wearing a tie
   D. He hadn't shaved

10. The 2022 follow-up to Prime Video's *Our Man in Japan* was supposed to see James May heading to the USA, but why was it changed at the last minute to take place in Italy?

    A. Budget restraints
    B. Covid restrictions
    C. Comments he'd made about the US
    D. Backlash on social media

The Idiot Box – Answers

1. C – A hermit living alone in the wilderness for forty years, seventy-four-year-old Smith travelled to Glasgow, and after taking a quick look around discreetly checked that it wasn't still 1981.

2. D – It was the accents. It's unclear exactly what Lord Sugar expected from a TV show set exclusively in Liverpool, but for some reason the vast majority of characters spoke with a mysterious Scouse twang.

3. C – It was Donald Trump's mate and star of *Borat 2*, Rudy Giuliani. The US version of *The Masked Singer* regularly attracts more than 4 million viewers – far more than the crowds he drew at his earlier gigs at Four Seasons Total Landscaping.

4. D – Richard Briers did appear in *Doctor Who*, but not as the legendary timelord. Richard Hurndall played the doctor just once – in 1983's 'The Five Doctors' – taking on the role of the first doctor as original actor William Hartnell had died eight years earlier.

5. A – A half-deflated netball to be precise, as it allowed just enough of a barrier between the, erm . . . moving parts. Spare a thought for the poor production runner with 'deep-cleaning the sex netball' on their CV.

6. A – Ed Balls was gifted a suitcase full of *Love Island* products as used on the show, including spray tan, fake eyelashes, and 350 STI test kits.

7. C – She paid tribute to music producer and HS2 hype man Pete Waterman. Burley did apologise and delete her tweet, but not before Education Secretary (yes, Education Secretary) Nadhim Zahawi replied to her, also offering a eulogy for the former *Pop Idol* judge.

8. C – It was *Celebrity Juice*, which ran for fourteen years after daring to ask the question 'what if there was an incredibly horny man for some reason?'

9. C – Beresford was criticised for not wearing a tie while reporting on the Jubilee, although in his defence it was A: 21 degrees in London and B: not the 1970s.

10. B – It was switched to *James May: Our Man in Italy* at the eleventh hour due to Covid restrictions making it too difficult to film in the US. That and the 90 per cent chance of getting shot in the face.

Socially Speaking – Round 1

Social media has given the world many things – poking, Farmville, President Donald Trump – but it mainly exists so that celebrities can makes fools of themselves on a daily basis. Can you work out who posted the following to their feeds in 2022?

1. PUTTING trump IN CHARGE OF AMERICA, IS LIKE PUTTING DRACULA IN CHARGE OF THE BLOOD BANK.

    A. Kanye West
    B. Cher
    C. Britney Spears
    D. Lindsay Lohan

2. #tbs That time I played Let It Be to Will Smith on Barry Manilow's piano. #NoBiggie.

    A. Ed Sheeran
    B. Joss Stone
    C. Piers Morgan
    D. Craig Charles

3. Yum 😋 Sweet and sour cow vagina.

    A. Right Said Fred

    B. Laurence Fox

    C. Jim Davidson

    D. Matt Le Tissier

4. FYI OUR SONS NAME ISN'T WOLF ANYMORE 😂😂 WE JUST REALLY DIDN'T FEEL LIKE IT WAS HIM. JUST WANTED TO SHARE BECAUSE I KEEP SEEING WOLF EVERYWHERE 🙏

    A. Kylie Jenner

    B. Kourtney Kardashian

    C. Kendall Jenner

    D. Khloé Kardashian

5. Get ready! Your favourite President will see you soon!

    A. Jair Bolsonaro

    B. Joe Biden

    C. Donald Trump

    D. Rudy Giuliani

6. LET'S GOOOOOOOO.

    A. Tyler the Creator

    B. Britney Spears

    C. The Weeknd

    D. Nicki Minaj

7. Here's a post of a picture of grass for no reason.

    A. Mark Hamill
    B. Samuel L. Jackson
    C. Natalie Portman
    D. Daisy Ridley

8. It is universally well known that mums have a thing for me. With Mother's Day fast approaching, why not give her a gift she can cherish forever? A video message from me!

    A. Paul Chuckle
    B. Bob Carolgees
    C. Chris Tarrant
    D. Nigel Farage

9. Ready to campaign in Keynsham but someone has pinched my coat.

    A. Diane Abbott
    B. Jacob Rees-Mogg
    C. Emily Thornberry
    D. Iain Duncan Smith

10. Yes! Sex can be fab at 60! What is so flipping shocking about that???

    A. Richard Madeley
    B. Dawn French
    C. Vanessa Feltz
    D. Jeremy Corbyn

SOCIALLY SPEAKING – ROUND 1 ANSWERS

1. B – Cher (Twitter – 12 January). Feels about five years too late, this. If only she could turn back time.

2. C – Piers Morgan (Instagram – 29 January). Morgan failed to see the irony of 'Let It Be' being performed by someone who's constantly outraged about everything.

3. A – Right Said Fred (Twitter – 24 February). Utterly bizarre, but in all honesty one of the more coherent things the 90s one-hit wonders tweeted in 2022.

4. A – Kylie Jenner (Instagram – 21 March). She revealed that she was changing her son's name because he no longer looked like a Wolf. Personally think she should have waited for another full moon to make sure.

5. C – Donald Trump (Truth Social – 14 February). Trump's first social media post in over a year was underwhelming compared to his tweets of old, but perhaps he's becoming more humble in his old age; after all, he didn't do something completely psychotic like name the platform after himself (looking at you Matt Hancock).

6. C – The Weeknd (Twitter – 24 February). An unremarkable tweet on the surface, but the Weeknd's timing couldn't have been worse, as his social media team posted this moments after news broke that Russia had launched its invasion of Ukraine.

7. A – It was Mark Hamill (Twitter – 25 February) who tweeted this. After a follower suggested he could tweet a picture of some grass and get thousands of likes, Hamill happily obliged (and in case you're wondering, the final figure was 22,000).

8. D – Nigel Farage (Twitter – 17 March). Never one to miss out on a quick buck, Nigel joined celebrity message service Thrillz to offer his services to millions of mums who couldn't quite afford one from Tom Hardy.

9. B – Jacob Rees-Mogg (Instagram – 26 February). Thankfully he was only joking, as the pockets contained a musket, classified papyrus scrolls and 12 oz of myrrh.

10. C – Vanessa Feltz (Instagram – 7 March). She claimed that it's perfectly acceptable to have sex at sixty, although police recommend pulling over to the hard shoulder first.

TILL DEATH (OR MESSY DIVORCE) DO US PART

After twenty-four months of cancellations and lost deposits due to the pandemic, 2022 was the year of the delayed wedding (and wondering why our suits had mysteriously shrunk). A number of famous faces also tied the knot, including Jennifer Lopez, John Cena and Boris Johnson (again). Can you work out the following famous brides and grooms from three-word clues and the date they got married?

1. Carriage, Wales, ears

    29 July 1981

2. Vegas, drummer, siblings

    15 May 2022

3. Ginger, Pope, head

    14 November 1532

4. Piano, sunglasses, Canada

    21 December 2014

5. Vampires, Scooby, wrestling

    1 September 2002

6. Thunder, short, Scientology

24 December 1990

7. Posh, thrones, bend

4 July 1999

8. Jungle, washboard, implants

10 September 2005

9. Yellow, vagina, Avengers

5 December 2003

10. Fresh, Matrix, slap

31 December 1997

Til Death (or Messy Divorce) Do Us Part – Answers

1. The wedding of **Diana Spencer** and future king of England **Charles Mountbatten-Windsor** was watched by a global audience of 750 million people. Forty-one years and 9,326 post office openings later, Prince Charles finally landed the top job in 2022.

2. Blink-182 drummer **Travis Barker** and famous-for-being-famous **Kourtney Kardashian** had not one, but three weddings in 2022. The first, an outrageously tacky one in Las Vegas, was followed by two traditional ceremonies, which were also unavoidably tacky due to the presence of Kourtney's family.

3. Henry Tudor and **Anne Boleyn**. Say what you will about Henry VIII but very few modern men are willing to fall out with the Pope and create a new offshoot of Christianity in the name of love. We'll admit he overreacted slightly with the break-up though.

4. Elton John and Canadian filmmaker husband **David Furnish** got married in 2014, although had been in a civil partnership since 2005. Elton John's current tour will purportedly be his last, coming as a huge relief to his autotune operator.

5. Sarah Michelle Gellar and **Freddie Prinze Jr** met on the set of *I Know What You Did Last Summer* but are more well-known for playing Daphne and Fred opposite a brown lump of CGI in the Scooby Doo live-action films.

6. Nicole Kidman tied the knot with pint-sized actor **Tom Cruise** in 1990 after they met while filming *Days of Thunder*. The pair separated in 2001 as the marriage was a distraction from Tom Cruise's quest to become the world's weirdest person.

7. David Beckham and **Victoria Adams** (now Beckham) celebrated their twenty-third wedding anniversary in July. Victoria reportedly turned down an eight-figure sum to join the most recent Spice Girls tour, despite organisers having no plans to turn her mic on.

8. Katie Price and **Peter Andre** married in 2005 after meeting on *I'm a Celebrity ... Get Me Out of Here!* the previous year. Thankfully neither are in the media much any more, although Peter Andre did receive a few column inches (pun intended) during the 'Wagatha Christie' libel case when comments made by Rebekah Vardy in 2004 comparing his manhood to 'a chipolata' resurfaced.

9. Chris Martin and **Gwyneth Paltrow** got married in 2003, although separated in 2014. In the years since, Gwyneth Paltrow has been hard at work creating candles that smell like vaginas – a difficult process which is very labia-intensive.

10. Will Smith and **Jada Pinkett**. Both of the elder Smiths have links to *The Matrix*, as Jada appeared in the second and third films in the franchise, whereas husband Will famously turned down the role of Neo, forcing them to take a chance on studious method actor Keanu Reeves instead.

NAME THAT MP – ROUND 1

Can you name the following currently serving MPs from their political timelines? (Constituencies, ministerial positions, and leadership roles)

1. MP for Chingford *(1992–1997)*

   MP for Chingford and Woodford Green *(1997– present)*
   Leader of the Opposition *(2001–2003)*
   Secretary of State for Work and Pensions *(2010–2016)*

2. MP for Doncaster North *(2005– present)*

   Minister for the Third Sector *(2006–2007)*
   Minister for the Cabinet Office, Chancellor of the Duchy of Lancaster *(2007–2008)*
   Secretary of State for Energy and Climate Change *(2008–2010)*
   Leader of the Opposition *(2010–2015)*
   Shadow Secretary of State for Business, Energy and Industrial Strategy *(2020–2021)*
   Shadow Secretary of State for Climate Change and Net Zero *(2021– present)*

3. MP for Wigan *(2010– present)*

   Shadow Minister for Children and Young Families *(2012–2013)*
   Shadow Minister for Civil Society *(2013–2015)*
   Shadow Secretary of State for Energy and Climate Change *(2015–2016)*
   Shadow Foreign Secretary *(2020–2021)*
   Shadow Secretary of State for Levelling Up, Housing and Communities *(2021– present)*

4. MP for Brighton Pavilion *(2010– present)*

   Leader of the Green Party of England and Wales *(2008–2012, 2016–2018)*

5. MP for Kingston and Surbiton *(1997–2015, 2017– present)*

   Parliamentary Under-Secretary of State for Employment Relations and Postal Affairs *(2010–2012)*
   Secretary of State for Energy and Climate Change *(2012–2015)*
   Deputy Leader of the Liberal Democrats *(2019–2020)*
   Leader of the Liberal Democrats *(2020– present)*

Name that MP – Round 1 Answers

1. Iain Duncan Smith

2. Ed Miliband

3. Lisa Nandy

4. Caroline Lucas

5. Ed Davey

At Labour's annual Halloween costume party, Keir Starmer came last after going as 'lectern with throwaway slogan' for the third year in a row:

2022 GENERAL KNOWLEDGE – ROUND 2

More 2022 miscellany to muse upon . . .

1. Which sporting figure appeared on *Good Morning Britain* in June to declare that they'd 'take a bullet' for Vladimir Putin?

    A. Dennis Rodman
    B. Matt Le Tissier
    C. Bernie Ecclestone
    D. Barry Fry

2. In March the government revealed that it would do what with five hundred lorryloads of PPE a month?

    A. Donate it to other countries
    B. Burn it
    C. Try to get a refund
    D. Bury it at a landfill site

3. Which band became the first to play a concert at Tottenham's £1 billion stadium in 2022?

    A. Coldplay
    B. Metallica
    C. Guns N' Roses
    D. Muse

4. Over the summer, a 'wet wipe island' the size of two tennis courts appeared in which UK river?

   A. Thames
   B. Mersey
   C. Trent
   D. Severn

5. In May, police arrested two teenagers at Gloucester services on suspicion of stealing £120,000 worth of what?

   A. Socks
   B. Dog food
   C. Chewing gum
   D. Manure

6. In May, Australian food chain Karen's Diner opened its first UK restaurant (in Sheffield, of all places) but what makes the experience unique?

   A. The staff are intentionally rude
   B. You have to cook the food yourself
   C. All the ingredients are past their sell-by date
   D. It only accepts cryptocurrency as payment

7. During Fashion Week in Paris, Kim Kardashian wore a Balenciaga bodysuit with a list of place names on her famous bottom. Along with London, which other surprising UK location was featured?

    A. Bradford
    B. Nottingham
    C. Barnsley
    D. Preston

8. In August, 103-year-old June Spencer from Nottingham retired from which profession?

    A. Cruise ship singer
    B. Life drawing model
    C. Soap actress
    D. Mechanic

9. During the great two-day heatwave of 2022 in July, what priceless advice did health bosses bestow upon the public?

    A. Stay hydrated by drinking water
    B. Avoid heatwave deaths by staying safe
    C. Don't look at the sun with binoculars
    D. Avoid wearing too many layers

10. A bizarre TikTok trend over the summer saw groups of people donning suits and tuxedos to attend screenings of which children's film?

    A. *DC League of Super-Pets*

    B. *Lightyear*

    C. *Minions: Rise of Gru*

    D. *Sonic the Hedgehog 2*

2022 General Knowledge – Round 2 Answers

1. C – Bernie Ecclestone said he'd take a bullet for Putin, as well as describing him as 'sensible', a 'first-class person' and someone who believed he was 'doing the right thing for Russia', before performing a screeching U-turn that most F1 drivers would be proud of and issuing a grovelling apology, saying he sympathised with Ukrainian people as he grew up during 'the war' – presumably the American civil one.

2. B – Five hundred lorryloads of PPE is being burned every month due to being unusable. Not great for the environment but at least it's one way to tackle the energy crisis.

3. C – Guns N' Roses played the first ever concert at Tottenham Hotspur Stadium. Fans were left disappointed after delays and sound issues, and the show was temporarily paused after Harry Kane instinctively fell over in the penalty area.

4. A – The giant island made mostly of wet wipes appeared in the Thames. It was eventually broken down and removed, but not before several MPs attempted to set up offshore trusts on it.

5. C – The pair were arrested on suspicion of stealing £120,000 worth of chewing gum. Officers say they became suspicious when a routine breathalyser showed dangerously high traces of spearmint and juicy fruit.

6. A – The staff at Karen's Diner are intentionally rude to customers, although for those on a budget, the cheapest way to get screamed at while eating is to go to Wetherspoons and mention the EU.

7. C – It was Barnsley that received the questionable honour of being displayed on someone's arse for a couple of hours, although in a somewhat anticlimactic explanation, it was revealed the locations were simply the birthplaces of Balenciaga staff. Bosses at the company later said that if they'd known the bodysuit would be worn by Kim Kardashian they'd have hired someone from Llanfairpwllgwyngyllgogerychwyrndrobwllllantysiliogogogoch.

8. C – She was a soap actress. June Spencer retired in 2022, having played Peggy Woolley in *The Archers* since 1950, although she is expected to reconsider the decision when she receives her winter heating bill.

9. B – Health bosses urged the public to 'avoid heatwave deaths by staying safe'. Who knows how many lives were saved by this incredible piece of advice, but most projections place it somewhere between zero and one.

10. C – It was *Minions: The Rise of Gru*. Many cinemas offered refunds to people unimpressed with the rowdy gatherings, although it's a bit odd complaining you've had an unpleasant experience when you've willingly paid money to see a Minions film.

178

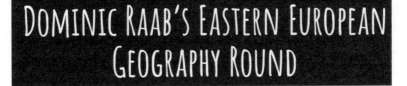

DOMINIC RAAB'S EASTERN EUROPEAN GEOGRAPHY ROUND

For many, one of the most surprising things about the Russia/Ukraine conflict was just how unfamiliar we are with the topography of Eastern Europe. Can you name the seven countries that border Ukraine? We've provided clues below but double points if you can name them using just the map.

1. Fifth largest population in the European Union. Played an unwilling role in the beginning of the Second World War.

2. The only country in Europe officially using the death penalty. Led by a good friend of Putin who vaguely resembles René Artois from *'Allo 'Allo!*

3. Already the world's largest country, but seems hell-bent on being even bigger. Bit nippy in the north so big coat is a must.

4. The world's largest per-capita car producer, and home to no fewer than eight UNESCO World Heritage Sites.

5. The official language is considered to be one of the hardest in Europe to learn, owning to its alphabet having forty-four letters. Its Prime Minister is firmly on the right side of the political spectrum.

6. Jeremy Clarkson once claimed it has the best road for driving in the world. You also run the risk of bumping into Dracula.

7. One of Europe's lesser-known countries, despite being larger (in terms of area) than Belgium, Cyprus and Slovenia. They always seem to pop up in England's World Cup qualifying group.

Dominic Raab's Eastern European Geography Round – Answers

1. Poland

2. Belarus

3. Russia

4. Slovakia

5. Hungary

6. Romania

7. Moldova

Justice Secretary Dominic Raab was urged to intervene after a man found to be complicit in blowing up a planet got off with forty hours of community service in Basildon:

ONE NIGHT IN TURIN

Hell well and truly froze over in 2022 as the UK not only received points at Eurovision, but finished the night on the hallowed left side of the screen after Sam Ryder's song 'Space Man' placed second behind Ukraine's Kalush Orchestra. To celebrate this historic silver medal, here are the titles of ten past UK entries, but can you remember who performed them?

1. 'Ooh Aah . . . Just a Little Bit' *(1996)*

    A. Sonia

    B. Love City Groove

    C. Katrina and the Waves

    D. Gina G

2. 'One Step Out of Time' *(1992)*

    A. Michael Ball

    B. Samantha Janus

    C. Imaani

    D. Frances Ruffelle

3. 'Embers' *(2021)*

    A. Lucie Jones

    B. Michael Rice

    C. James Newman

    D. James Fox

4. 'Save Your Kisses for Me' *(1976)*

    A. The Shadows
    B. Black Lace
    C. The New Seekers
    D. Brotherhood of Man

5. 'Cry Baby' *(2003)*

    A. Jemini
    B. Javine
    C. Precious
    D. Josh Dubovie

6. 'Love Will Set You Free' *(2012)*

    A. Scooch
    B. Engelbert Humperdinck
    C. Jade Ewen
    D. Jessica Garlick

7. 'Congratulations' *(1968)*

    A. Kenneth McKellar
    B. Cliff Richard
    C. Matt Monro
    D. The New Seekers

8. 'Boom Bang-a-Bang' *(1969)*

    A. Sandie Shaw
    B. Kathy Kirby
    C. Lulu
    D. Olivia Newton-John

9. 'I Can' *(2011)*

    A. Bonnie Tyler
    B. Andy Abraham
    C. Joe and Jake
    D. Blue

10. 'All' *(1957)*

    A. Patricia Bredin
    B. Bryan Johnson
    C. Matt Monro
    D. Cliff Richard

One Night in Turin – Answers

1. D – Australian Gina G (real name Gina Gardiner) placed eighth in 1996 with the lyrically ambiguous 'Ooh Aah … Just a Little Bit', and despite being considered a bit of a one-hit-wonder, achieved five top-forty singles in the UK before retiring to become a pub quiz answer.

2. A – Nothing says 'European party anthem' like veteran crooner Michael Ball, who finished second in 1992, and might have won had fans not been disappointed by the absence of Tommy Cannon.

3. C – James Newman represented the UK in 2021 with 'Embers', which were all that remained when our hopes of receiving a single point went up in flames.

4. D – Brotherhood of Man's sickly sweet 'Save Your Kisses for Me' narrowly won the 1976 contest and holds the record for the highest-selling Eurovision-winning song of all time after shifting six million copies worldwide. Ah – such innocent times, when singing about kissing a three-year-old could be delivered in all sincerity and without comment.

5. A – One of the most infamous (and out-of-tune) performances in the competition's history, Jemini received the UK's first ever 'nul points' at the 2003 contest in Latvia. The media at the time suggested it was due to a backlash over the Iraq war, but incredibly, the threat of placing last at Eurovision did little – if anything – to sway Tony Blair on foreign policy.

6. B – Up-and-coming pop sensation Engelbert Humperdinck was the UK's entry in 2012. He briefly held the title of oldest entrant in Eurovision history (seventy-six), before fellow sep-tuagenarian Natalya Pugachyova swooped in later that same evening to claim it for Russia, a bit like Vladimir Putin with Crimea and the Donbas.

7. B – It was of course Cliff Richard, who lost by a single point to Spanish entry 'La, la, la', although he probably would have won if not for the appalling dancing at the end.

8. C – Lulu's victory in 1969 was a four-way tie with France, Spain and the Netherlands. She would go on to encapsulate the true spirit of Eurovision by telling John Peel, 'I know it's a rotten song, but I won, so who cares?' Fans of Lulu's trenchant observations will no doubt have enjoyed her commentary on the Jubilee Pageant, which included such gems as 'I remember Mr Whippy'.

9. D – The approach of entering an already-established act paid off for the UK in 2011 after the points tally for Blue's 'I Can' hit triple figures. (Well, just about. They received one hundred points to finish eleventh.)

10. A – A tough one this, but Patricia Bredin was the UK's first ever entrant back in 1957, placing seventh with six points. The first and third Eurovision Song Contests were the only ones that the UK didn't enter, and – for better or worse – we've been involved every year since 1959.

ANY OLD EXCUSE

This round is all about excuses, and there were some cracking ones in 2022. How many of the following dubious claims do you remember?

1. What did Joe Biden say caused him to fall off his bike while cycling in Delaware in June?

    A.   A raccoon ran in front of him
    B.   His helmet slipped over his eyes
    C.   His front wheel buckled
    D.   His feet got stuck in the pedals

2. After losing via knockout to Tyson Fury in their world title match at Wembley, why did Dillian Whyte claim that he should have been given 'extra time to recover'?

    A.   The bell had gone
    B.   Fury pushed him
    C.   Fans were shining lasers
    D.   He hit the turnbuckle

3. In late April, Tory MP Neil Parish resigned after being caught watching porn in the House of Commons, but in a subsequent interview what did he claim he was actually trying to look up online?

    A. Caravans

    B. Washing machines

    C. Tractors

    D. Traction engines

4. For reasons known only to himself, a friend of Parish publicly backed him up by claiming the story was true, and that the MP was searching for a model called what?

    A. Mistress

    B. Dominator

    C. Backhoe Loader

    D. Big Daddy

5. Elon Musk slammed the brakes on his Twitter takeover in May after claiming to have reservations about what?

    A. Regional free speech laws

    B. Plummeting share prices

    C. The number of bot accounts

    D. The company's servers

6. In April it was revealed that Angela Rayner was present at the event where Keir Starmer was photographed drinking a beer during lockdown. Why did Labour say they'd previously claimed she wasn't there?

    A. It was a clerical error
    B. They thought she was in Wales
    C. It was a 'genuine mistake'
    D. It was Jeremy Corbyn's fault

7. Which celebrity chef accused Boris Johnson of using the cost-of-living crisis as an excuse for not tackling obesity?

    A. Jamie Oliver
    B. Gordon Ramsay
    C. Nigella Lawson
    D. James Martin

8. During an interview following Liverpool's Champions League semi-final win over Villarreal, pundit Thierry Henry was left red-faced when Virgil van Dijk accused him of not returning his texts. What was Henry's excuse for the snub?

    A. He was in the bath
    B. He'd changed his number
    C. He was filming a Renault Clio ad
    D. He couldn't be bothered to reply

9. What did Rishi Sunak say prevented him from further raising benefits in his 2022 spring budget statement?

    A. A lack of public support

    B. The war in Ukraine

    C. Decades-old Labour debts

    D. Old computer software

10. In June, former heavyweight boxer Mike Tyson was filmed punching a fellow passenger while on a flight to Florida. What reason did he give for the violent reaction?

    A. The back of his seat was being kicked

    B. The guy 'crossed a line'

    C. He was 'high and pissed off'

    D. He was trying to watch *Jurassic World*

ANY OLD EXCUSE – ANSWERS

1. D – He said his feet got stuck in the toe straps as he came to a stop. Republicans were quick to point out that Donald Trump never fell off his bike, but then it's significantly more difficult when the stabilisers are on.

2. B – Whyte claimed that the push – after receiving an uppercut from Fury – was the reason he lost, and not the fact that stewards had to retrieve his head from Watford.

3. C – Parish claimed to be looking at tractors before moving on to various other things getting ploughed.

4. B – Colin Slade – a county councillor from Devon – claimed Parish was looking for a tractor model called 'Dominator', thereby carrying on the theme of agricultural machinery by digging him into an even deeper hole.

5. C – Musk – somewhat ironically, given his penchant for AI and robotics – claimed to have reservations about the number of bot accounts on the platform, although he was quickly reassured by legal experts @lawyer232094, @lawyer9548983 and @Horny_Milf_1972

6. C – They claimed it was a 'genuine mistake'. Presumably the same 'genuine mistakes' they spent the first half of the year demanding other people resign over.

7. A – The government drew Jamie Oliver's ire after a U-turn on banning buy-one-get-one-free offers for unhealthy food. Tesco and Sainsbury's decided to ban the offers anyway, as it greatly reduced the risk of having to listen to Jamie Oliver again.

8. B – Henry said he didn't reply because he'd changed his number, although fellow pundit Graeme Souness instinctively claimed it was all Paul Pogba's fault.

9. D – After blaming old computer software for the lack of support, Sunak was compared to the 'computer says no' character from *Little Britain*, although Matt Lucas and David Walliams were quick to argue they'd never write anything that stupid or offensive.

10. C – Tyson told Jimmy Kimmel he usually copes with overenthusiastic fans very well but on this occasion he was 'irritated, tired, high and pissed off'. Luckily, fellow passengers calmed him down before 'human ear' joined chicken and beef on the in-flight menu.

THE OBLIGATORY SPORTS ROUND

Because let's face it, it wouldn't be a quiz without one. See how you fare with these sporting questions from 2022.

1. At the World Snooker Championship in April, a match between Mark Selby and Yan Bingtao was halted when play was interrupted by what?

    A. A dog
    B. A mouse
    C. A streaker
    D. A pigeon

2. Why was twenty-five-year-old club runner Ellis Cross shocked after winning the 2022 Vitality London 10k?

    A. He'd taken a wrong turn
    B. It was his first ever race
    C. He beat Mo Farah
    D. He broke the British 10k record

3. Ex-golfer Greg Norman veered wildly out of his lane and sparked outrage in May when he said 'Look, we've all made mistakes' while talking about what?

    A. 9/11

    B. The Kennedy assassination

    C. The murder of Jamal Khashoggi

    D. The Khmer Rouge

4. During the 2022 Monaco Historic Grand Prix, Charles Leclerc crashed a 1974 Ferrari that had been driven by which F1 legend?

    A. Niki Lauda

    B. James Hunt

    C. Mario Andretti

    D. Emerson Fittipaldi

5. 2022 marked the highly anticipated return of the world-famous cheese rolling at Cooper's Hill, which can be found in which county?

    A. Worcestershire

    B. Herefordshire

    C. Gloucestershire

    D. Wiltshire

6. Eyebrows were raised when world number one Ashleigh Barty sensationally quit tennis, but just two weeks later she entered – and won – a competition in which other sport?

    A. Rowing
    B. Cycling
    C. Swimming
    D. Golf

7. One of the most shocking sporting moments of 2022 was the untimely passing of cricket legend Shane Warne. During the first Test of the 1993 Ashes he produced the so-called 'ball of the century', but which unlucky batsman was on the receiving end?

    A. Mike Gatting
    B. Ian Botham
    C. Mike Atherton
    D. Graham Gooch

8. A Cambridgeshire Live article on 19 May claimed that the Queen was partial to which sporting video game?

    A. *FIFA*
    B. *Wii Sports*
    C. *Mario Kart*
    D. *Tony Hawk's Pro Skater*

9. In 2022 it was announced that the horse-riding section of the pentathlon could be replaced by what?

    A. Cycling

    B. Archery

    C. Fishing

    D. An obstacle course

10. What complaint did Rafael Nadal and Novak Djokovic have about their French open quarter-final on 1 June?

    A. The ball boys were too slow

    B. The net was too dark

    C. The umpire was too quiet

    D. It finished too late

The Obligatory Sports Round – Answers

1. D – Play between Selby and Bingtao was halted when a pigeon landed on the table, possibly after hearing that both players were seeded.

2. C – Ellis Cross – who runs for Aldershot, Farnham and District and paid £37 to enter the event – beat Mo Farah by four seconds, finishing in 28:40. After the win, Cross set his sights on the ultimate prize in British distance running: flogging Quorn sausages on the telly.

3. C – Norman was speaking at a golfing event in Saudi Arabia when he was asked about the 2018 killing of Jamal Khashoggi, and realistically it went about as well as asking a retired golfer about foreign affairs can go.

4. A – Leclerc was driving Lauda's 1974 Ferrari when he spun out and crashed into the barrier. It was valued at roughly £1 million, so fortunately it was one of the cheaper cars at Monte Carlo.

5. C – Hundreds of people flocked to Gloucestershire to chase a wheel of cheese down a hill, which due to spiralling food costs was a Mini Babybel.

6. D – Barty won the ladies' championship at Brookwater Golf and Country Club, and it can't be said that she's in it for the money as she took home just $30, which at the time was around £17.

7. A – Mike Gatting was the unlucky batsman when Warne defied the laws of physics with his first ball in his first Ashes Test. The cricketing legend went out in true Shane Warne fashion in 2022 after ordering a made-to-measure suit and being visited by an unspecified number of masseuses at a luxury resort in Thailand.

8. B – It's claimed that her majesty is partial to a bit of *Wii Sports* bowling after Kate bought William a Nintendo Wii back in 2008. The article also states she hates playing *Monopoly*, presumably as players have to pay rent and there's no option to buy yourself out of jail with £12 million.

9. D – Calls to replace the horse-riding portion with an obstacle course are part of plans to elevate pentathlon from the Olympic event nobody cares about to the Olympic event nobody cares about but with an obstacle course.

10. D – Both players claimed that the match finished too late after Nadal won in four sets at 1.15 a.m. local time, although fans in attendance said it was worth missing the last train home to see Djokovic lose at the most inconvenient time possible.

WHATEVER YOU DO, DON'T MENTION THE SPECIAL MILITARY OPERATION – ROUND 2

In a perfect world, this story wouldn't have lasted long enough to warrant more than one round, but unfortunately it continued to dominate the news cycle for the whole of 2022.

1. Which businessman challenged Putin to a fight, with Ukraine at stake?

    A. Richard Branson
    B. Jeff Bezos
    C. Elon Musk
    D. Alan Sugar

2. On 12 March, a Russian demonstrator in Nizhny Novgorod was arrested for holding up a sign that said what?

    A. 'No war'
    B. 'They're lying to you'
    C. 'Peace'
    D. Absolutely nothing

3. On 18 March, Putin held a pro-war rally, which according to the Kremlin was attended by how many people?

    A. 50,000

    B. 100,000

    C. 150,000

    D. 200,000

4. One of the most cringeworthy moments of the conflict arrived during a St Patrick's Day lunch in Washington when Nancy Pelosi read aloud a poem about Ukraine, sent to her by which musician?

    A. Bono

    B. Enya

    C. Bob Geldof

    D. Sinéad O'Connor

5. During a summit in Tehran on 20 July to discuss the ongoing war, which world leader left Vladimir Putin awkwardly waiting in front of the camera for almost a minute?

    A. Xi Jinping

    B. Recep Erdoğan

    C. Aleksandr Lukashenko

    D. Emmanuel Macron

6. An anti-war video that directly addressed Putin went viral on social media after being recorded by which Hollywood megastar?

   A. Meryl Streep
   B. Arnold Schwarzenegger
   C. Tom Hanks
   D. Dwayne Johnson

7. When three Russian cosmonauts arrived on the International Space Station in late March, what was notable about their uniforms?

   A. They displayed the peace symbol
   B. They said 'NO WAR'
   C. The Russian flags had been removed
   D. They were yellow and blue

8. As the sanctions continued to pile up, Russia caused a few billion raised eyebrows by inexplicably applying to host which sporting event?

   A. 2028 Olympic Games
   B. 2023 World Chess Championship
   C. Euro 28
   D. 2030 World Cup

9. Which ageing rocker branded Joe Biden a 'war criminal' for his involvement in the Russia/Ukraine conflict during his 2022 North American tour?

    A. Bob Dylan
    B. Roger Waters
    C. John Lydon
    D. Eric Clapton

10. Which actor, who became a Russian citizen in 2013, angered the Kremlin in early April by accusing Putin of 'crazy, unacceptable excesses' in Ukraine?

    A. Gerard Depardieu
    B. Steven Seagal
    C. Randy Quaid
    D. Sarah Lancashire

Whatever You Do, Don't Mention the Special Military Operation – Round 2 Answers

1. C – Presumably frustrated by the amount of attention the war was taking away from him, Musk challenged the Russian President to 'single combat' which, had it taken place, would have been the only possible scenario in which the West would have cheered on Putin.

2. D – Footage went viral after police arrested a demonstrator holding up . . . a blank piece of paper. Unconfirmed reports suggest they were handed A4 day prison sentence.

3. D – 200,000 people allegedly attended the 'concert' at Moscow's Luzhniki Stadium, which is especially impressive given that it has a capacity of 81,000.

4. A – The U2 frontman sapped the world's last remaining drops of serotonin with a poem that that likened the Ukraine situation to Saint Patrick driving out the snakes from Ireland. Still, at least we weren't subjected to a 'where the streets are Ukraine' charity single.

5. B – It was Turkey's Recep Erdoğan who was fashionably late to the meeting with Vladimir Putin in July, leaving the Russian President shuffling his feet for more than fifty seconds. Putin laughed it off, but told Erdoğan to let the KGB know next time he was on the roof of a tall building during high winds.

6. B – The actor-turned-politician warned Russians that they were being lied to before telling Putin, 'You started this war, and you can stop it'. After it didn't really achieve anything, military experts urged him to go one step further and threaten another *Jingle All the Way* sequel.

7. D – The cosmonauts entered the ISS wearing the colours of the Ukrainian flag. According to Russia it was purely a coincidence and the uniforms had been packed months beforehand, which is fair enough given the Kremlin's impeccable history of telling the truth.

8. C – Russia decided it was worth a shot to apply to host the Euros in the middle of a military conflict. To be fair, if you discount minor setbacks such as travel bans, financial sanctions, political unrest, lack of places to eat and the fact Russia couldn't even take part, it was a worthwhile endeavour.

9. B – As part of the stage show for his tour, former Pink Floyd frontman Roger Waters included a graphic reading 'WAR CRIMINAL' over a photograph of Joe Biden. In a follow-up interview with CNN he also criticised Volodymyr Zelenskyy and described Taiwan as part of China, although having previously disputed the need for teachers and education it's unclear if he knows what he's talking about.

10. A – Depardieu had his passport presented to him in 2013 during a meeting with Vladimir Putin, although unfortunately it expired in the time it took to slide across his massive table.

COURT IN THE ACT

If 2022's 'Wagatha Christie' court case between Rebekah Vardy and Colleen Rooney taught us anything (aside from being the most inept nickname for anything ever) it's that courtroom sketches are invariably awful. Can you identify the following famous names from their hastily drawn mugs?

1.

2.

3.

4.

5.

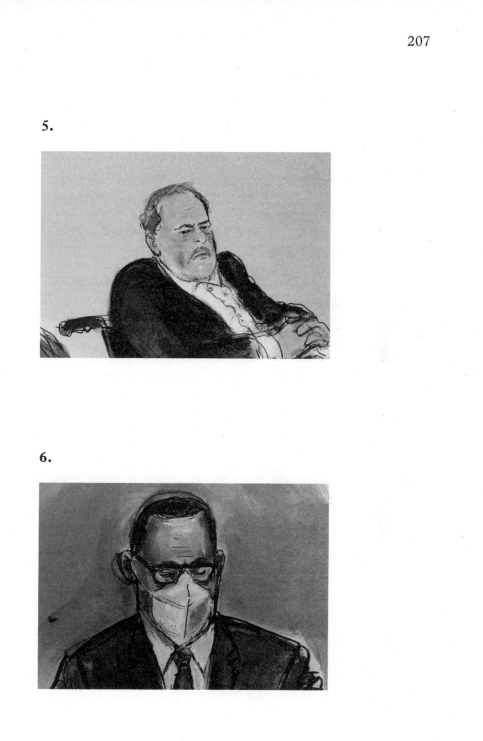

6.

Court in the Act – Answers

1. Kim Kardashian, appearing in court after reality star Blac Chyna accused her family of destroying her TV career.

2. Disgraced former socialite **Ghislaine Maxwell**, during her sex-trafficking trial in New York.

3. Adult film actress and thorn in Donald Trump's side **Stormy Daniels**, appearing at celebrity lawyer Michael Avenatti's fraud trial early in the year.

4. American actor **Jussie Smollett**, who was found guilty on five of six charges after being accused of staging an attack on himself and then lying to police about it.

5. Former film producer and convicted sex offender **Harvey Weinstein** at his sentencing hearing in Manhattan.

6. Singer **R. Kelly**, sketched at the moment a jury found him guilty on eight counts of sex trafficking and one of racketeering.

Wayne Rooney looked bored to tears throughout his wife's libel case, often passing the time by making detailed sketches, one of which we can exclusively reveal for the first time:

MISSING WORDS – ROUND 2

You know the drill – ten headlines, but each has a key bit of information missing.

1. You can name a _____ after your ex for Valentine's Day at this Kent zoo
    Metro – 14 February

    A. Rat
    B. Cockroach
    C. Weasel
    D. Snake

2. Camila Cabello rebounds from accidental _____ on live TV
    Los Angeles Times – 8 March

    A. Headbutt
    B. Fart
    C. Front flip
    D. Nudity

3. Naked man says he's _____, lives in woman's car trunk for days without 'saying a word'
Crime Online – 10 March

    A. JFK's twin
    B. The Pope's son
    C. Elvis Presley
    D. The second coming of Christ

4. Giant _____ declared largest on record – but here's why you wouldn't want to eat it
Sky News – 17 February

    A. Mushroom
    B. Doughnut
    C. Banana
    D. Strawberry

5. Former M&S cashier, 20, earns £50k in three months _____ in the nude
Wales Online – 3 April

    A. Playing video games
    B. Mowing people's lawns
    C. Eating Percy Pig sweets
    D. Reviewing art

6. Google Maps has started _____ to 'protect their privacy'
   Mirror – 15 March

   A. Blurring dogs' faces
   B. Removing celebrities' homes
   C. Hiding royal residences
   D. Obscuring people's house numbers

7. _____ posted through woman's letterbox in case of mistaken identity
   Metro – 9 March

   A. Fireworks
   B. Dog poo
   C. Pornography
   D. Dead bat

8. Border authorities find _____ hidden in man's clothing
   AP News – 9 March

   A. 28 spiders
   B. 52 reptiles
   C. 67 beetles
   D. A small child

9. The Dutch vow to egg Jeff Bezos' yacht if _____ to let his boat pass
   NPR – 9 February

   A. A reservoir is drained
   B. Endangered fish are killed
   C. A bridge is dismantled
   D. Curfew is imposed

10. Mathew Horne says it's hard _____ during the Ukraine war
    GB News – 17 March

    A. To stay positive
    B. Feeling powerless
    C. To focus on anything else
    D. Promoting *The Nan Movie*

MISSING WORDS – ROUND 2 ANSWERS

1. B – 'You can name a **cockroach** after your ex for Valentine's Day at this Kent zoo.' For just £1.50 Hemsley Conservation Centre lets spurned lovers name a roach after their old flames. The only downside is that in the event of surviving a nuclear apocalypse you still run the risk of being reminded of your ex.

2. D – 'Camila Cabello rebounds from accidental **nudity** on live TV.' During an interview on *The One Show*, the singer-songwriter suffered a Janet Jackson-style wardrobe malfunction while dancing. Any hope of not drawing too much attention to it quickly disappeared, as she was talking to fellow guest Alan Carr at the time.

3. B – 'Naked man says he's **the Pope's son**, lives in woman's car trunk for days without "saying a word".' The man was discovered in the trunk of a car by Canadian police. Photographs of the incident confirm that he was indeed nude, but the Vatican has thus far declined to comment on the Pope thing.

4. D – 'Giant **strawberry** declared largest on record – but here's why you wouldn't want to eat it.' The 289g fruit (or 'accessory fruit' for food pedants) was officially declared the world's largest, but was said to be no longer edible after being frozen for over a year, though that's exactly what you would say if you didn't want someone eating your massive strawberry.

5. C – 'Former M&S cashier, 20, earns £50k in three months **eating Percy Pig sweets** in the nude.' As the popularity of using food mascots for sexual gratification grew in 2022, a deeply concerned Colin the Caterpillar suddenly became very aware of his shape.

6. A – 'Google Maps has started **blurring dogs' faces** to "protect their privacy".' If only they could do something about dog faeces now.

7. D – '**Dead bat** posted through woman's letterbox in case of mistaken identity.' A good Samaritan in the town of Ramsbottom says she meant to post it to a neighbour who looks after sick bats. You could argue that being dead is one of the more serious ailments that a bat can have, and that's before being rammed through someone's front door.

8. B – 'Border authorities find **52 reptiles** hidden in man's clothing.' The animals were discovered as a thirty-year-old man tried to enter California from Mexico. Border police say they became suspicious that he might be concealing snakes when they noticed he dressed to the left and the right, and then three more times to the left.

9. C – 'The Dutch vow to egg Jeff Bezos' yacht if **a bridge is dismantled** to let his boat pass.' More than four thousand people in Rotterdam signed up to throw eggs at the retail billionaire's yacht if a historic bridge was dismantled to let it through, much in the same way your front door has to come off when the DVD you ordered from Amazon arrives in a sixty-foot box.

10. D – 'Mathew Horne says it's hard **promoting *The Nan Movie*** during the Ukraine war.' Although judging from the reviews, not as hard as actually watching it.

FACING THE MUSIC

After the entertainment industry was devastated by the pandemic, a small positive about 2022 was that musicians were finally able to resume doing weird stuff for our amusement.

1. Which singer sold two Banksy artworks in a Sotheby's auction for an eye-watering £7.2 million?

    A. Robbie Williams
    B. Madonna
    C. Mick Jagger
    D. Rod Stewart

2. Why was Kanye West's music video for 'Easy' roundly condemned?

    A. The dancers were completely nude
    B. It featured sacrilegious imagery
    C. He was depicted killing a love rival
    D. It referenced Jeffrey Epstein

3. In February, Trentham Monkey Forest in Stoke-on-Trent hired an impersonator of which musician to encourage their Barbary macaques to have sex?

    A. Marvin Gaye

    B. Tom Jones

    C. Ian Brown

    D. Barbra Streisand

4. Which Canadian musician removed his music from Spotify in protest at Covid-19 misinformation on the platform?

    A. Shawn Mendes

    B. Bryan Adams

    C. Neil Young

    D. Michael Bublé

5. Dr Dre headlined the Super Bowl halftime show, but which of the following rappers did NOT join him onstage?

    A. 50 Cent

    B. Jay-Z

    C. Eminem

    D. Snoop Dogg

6. How did Paul McCartney reveal he was headlining Glastonbury?

    A. Drone display
    B. TV ad during *Saturday Night Takeaway*
    C. With a fake Wordle result
    D. On *The Joe Rogan Experience* podcast

7. In March, Mick Jagger revealed he had written his first ever what?

    A. Cheque
    B. Opera
    C. Radio jingle
    D. TV theme

8. Which singer, already the youngest Record of the Year winner at the Grammys, also became the youngest person to headline Coachella in 2022?

    A. Lorde
    B. Dua Lipa
    C. Billie Eilish
    D. Doja Cat

9. What alliterative title did Harry Styles give to his third album, released in May?

    A. Harry's House
    B. Harry Houdini
    C. Hip Hip Hooray For Harry!
    D. Hungry Hungry Harry

10. Following in the footsteps of Dolly Parton, Lionel Richie and Tony Bennett, which singer occupied Glastonbury 2022's famous 'legends slot'?

  A. Barry Gibb
  B. Shirley Bassey
  C. Brian Wilson
  D. Diana Ross

FACING THE MUSIC – ANSWERS

1. A – The two pieces, *Vandalised Oils* and *Girl with Balloon*, sold for £4.4 million and £2.8 million respectively, and might have gone for much more had they not been owned by Robbie Williams.

2. C – West (or Ye as he likes people to call him now, but nobody does) was vocal about trying to win his ex-wife back, so naturally he filmed a video depicting the murder of her new boyfriend (*Saturday Night Live*'s Pete Davidson). Unbelievably, it didn't work and the pair divorced on 2 March.

3. A – They were serenaded by a Marvin Gaye impersonator. If you're ever having a rough day, just be thankful you're not in Stoke singing 'Let's Get it On' to a monkey. Actually, just be thankful you're not in Stoke.

4. C – The 'Heart of Gold' singer demanded the platform remove his catalogue due to vaccine misinformation on *The Joe Rogan Experience* podcast – not the first time he's spoken up about the needle and the damage done.

5. B – Jay-Z was the only artist not to join Dre onstage. The legendary producer was however joined by rap royalty Snoop Dogg, Eminem, Mary J. Blige, 50 Cent and Kendrick Lamar, although Super Bowl organisers quickly regretted booking Dr Dre after the majority of viewers instantly forgot about him.

6. C – McCartney used word-guessing game Wordle to reveal he was returning to the Pyramid Stage – in the process becoming the first headliner to predate the actual pyramids.

7. D – The then-seventy-eight-year-old Rolling Stones front-man wrote the theme for espionage series *Slow Horses*. The show stars Gary Oldman, and, with the inclusion of Jagger, very old man.

8. C – Eilish received rave reviews for her performance at the legendary California festival, but spare a thought for Damon Albarn, who joined her onstage and was mistaken by fans for her dad.

9. A – If it was ever in doubt, Harry cemented his status as the ex-boyband member people can actually remember, like Robbie Williams, or Ronan Keating, or the big one from Westlife who went out with the woman who won *The Masked Singer*.

10. D – Glastonbury continued with its tradition of sticking someone who hasn't really done anything since the 80s on the Pyramid Stage and hoping everyone's too pissed to notice, after the success of Jeremy Corbyn in 2017.

MATT HANCOCK V2

After a calamitous 2021 which saw Matt Hancock step down as Health Secretary following *that* breach of Covid guidelines, 2022's biggest PR campaign saw the launch of Matt Hancock v2 – which was exactly the same as the old one except he began wearing a turtleneck. Let's see how well you know the Poundland Casanova of British politics.

1. Matt Hancock's relaunch suffered an early setback in February when High Court judges ruled that he acted unlawfully when he ...

   A. Took shares in his sister's company
   B. Kissed an aide in a restricted area
   C. Failed to protect care-home residents
   D. Appointed people to top Covid jobs

2. How did Hancock defend kissing aide Gina Coladangelo while social-distancing rules were still in place?

   A. He wasn't aware he broke the rules
   B. He 'fell in love'
   C. He didn't know they were on camera
   D. They didn't use tongues

3. In March, Hancock heroically returned to his constituency to oppose a new what?

    A. Renewable energy farm

    B. Children's hospital

    C. Sensory garden

    D. Art gallery

4. How did he offer to help Ukrainian refugees?

    A. By offering free health advice

    B. By donating his MP salary

    C. By letting them live in his house

    D. By driving supplies to Poland

5. Hancock found himself in hot water again when the National Audit Office found that he'd failed to disclose an exchange of messages with whom?

    A. Owen Paterson

    B. Chris Whitty

    C. Sajid Javid

    D. Babestation

6. Writing for the *Mail on Sunday* in late March, what did Hancock claim people kept asking him?

    A. To run for PM

    B. For a selfie

    C. If there would be more lockdowns

    D. For his phone number

7. Writing for the *Telegraph*, Hancock said it was 'out of date' for recruiters to reject CVs that contain what?

    A. Exaggerated claims

    B. Typos

    C. Crude language

    D. No mention of references

8. Signs that Hancock might enjoy the limelight a bit too much have always been there of course. In 2018 he became the first MP to launch his own app, but what was it called?

    A. Matt Hancock MP

    B. InstaHan

    C. MattSpace

    D. FaceCock

9. Just before Easter it was revealed that the University of Manchester was to award Hancock an honorary degree for his commitment to the UK during the Covid-19 pandemic, but why didn't he accept it?

    A. He said he didn't deserve it

    B. Students protested against it

    C. It meant going to Manchester

    D. It was an April Fool's joke

10. When police confirmed that an initial twenty people had been fined for parties at Downing Street during lockdown, Hancock said Boris Johnson should:

    A. Resign

    B. Not resign

    C. Apologise

    D. Ignore them, they're just jealous x

MATT HANCOCK V2 – ANSWERS

1. D – Courts found that the government hadn't complied with public sector equality duty when making top Covid appointments, as they should have also considered applicants who weren't donors or mates.

2. B – The former Health Secretary told the *Diary of a CEO* podcast he broke the rules because he fell in love. Not sure where 'trying to get your leg over' was on the list of Covid exemptions. Must have been towards the back.

3. A – He declared his opposition to a 2,700-acre solar farm, presumably due to the risk of it being used to power CCTV cameras.

4. C – He offered to house up to seven refugees. It's impossible to comprehend the horror of fleeing a warzone only to find yourself in Matt Hancock's spare room wondering why there's a mirror on the ceiling.

5. A – It was former Northern Ireland Secretary Owen Paterson, who, despite spending twenty-four years as an MP, went on to cement his legacy as 'that bloke who resigned over lobbying for healthcare and sausages'.

6. C – Hancock confidently claimed there would be no more lockdowns due to his expert handling of the pandemic, and not because the government's non-stop partying meant no one would take any notice of new rules anyway.

7. B – It was typos, although to be fair to Hancock he was speaking in support of people with dyslexia. Recruiters have of course been known to overlook other things on CVs, such as suitability and relevant experience – for example, when he nearly landed that top job at the UN.

8. A – It was called Matt Hancock MP. The app didn't exactly set the world on fire and hasn't been updated in quite some time, meaning that anyone wanting to connect with Matt Hancock will have to do so the old-fashioned way and join Tinder.

9. D – It was an April Fool's joke, which rendered the gesture completely worthless; a bit like working for the NHS and being rewarded with claps.

10. B – He said the PM shouldn't resign, after realising the longer this partygate thing rumbles on the more Matt Hancock gets to go on the telly to talk about his favourite subject, Matt Hancock.

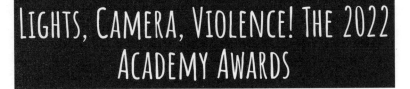

LIGHTS, CAMERA, VIOLENCE! THE 2022 ACADEMY AWARDS

Despite 'that incident' snagging most of the headlines, some other stuff also happened at the world's most famous awards ceremony. How much can you remember about the night that inspired a million memes?

1. After the ceremony, ex-One Direction member Liam Payne resurfaced to share his thoughts on the altercation between Will Smith and Chris Rock (it's unclear who asked) but why did the interview cause widespread confusion?

    A. He'd shaved his eyebrows off

    B. His accent had changed

    C. He'd developed a lisp

    D. His front teeth were missing

2. The 2022 awards marked the first appearance of the 'Fan Favourite Award', which allowed films that people actually had fun watching to pick up a consolation prize. Which film won?

    A. *Spider-Man: No Way Home*

    B. *Jackass Forever*

    C. *Army of the Dead*

    D. *Venom: Let There Be Carnage*

3. Over on the red carpet, Kristen Stewart was accused of 'ripping up the rule book' by wearing what?

    A. Shorts
    B. A baseball cap
    C. Trainers
    D. Lederhosen

4. Comedian Amy Schumer took a shot at which A-lister with the line 'He's done so much to fight climate change and leave behind a cleaner, greener planet for his girlfriends'?

    A. Jerry Seinfeld
    B. Sean Penn
    C. Leonardo DiCaprio
    D. Matt Damon

5. The Golden Raspberries, or 'The Razzies' are held on the same weekend as the Oscars and celebrate the worst films and performances of the year, but in 2022 which actor was given not only their own award, but their very own category?

    A. Steven Seagal
    B. Nicolas Cage
    C. Bruce Willis
    D. John Cusack

6. And speaking of the Razzies, which cinematic masterpiece swept the board, winning five of the night's top prizes?

    A. *Space Jam: A New Legacy*

    B. *Diana: The Musical*

    C. *The Woman in the Window*

    D. *Infinite*

7. Ahead of the Oscars, what did Sean Penn threaten to do if the Academy didn't allow Ukrainian president Volodymyr Zelenskyy to address the audience?

    A. Donate his Oscars to Ukraine

    B. Storm the stage

    C. Block the red carpet

    D. Destroy his Oscar statuettes

8. In the days following the Oscars every celebrity on the planet lined up to share their thoughts on the Will Smith incident. How did Daniel Radcliffe say he felt when asked about it on *Good Morning Britain*?

    A. 'Stupendously fatigued'

    B. 'Dramatically bored'

    C. 'Completely indifferent'

    D. 'I blame J.K. Rowling'

9. Five days after the ceremony, Smith announced that he was doing what?

    A. Resigning from the Academy

    B. Handing back his Oscar

    C. Attending anger management

    D. Retiring from acting

10. What was legendary composer Hans Zimmer wearing when he accepted his Oscar for best original score?

    A. A kilt

    B. A kimono

    C. A bathrobe

    D. A medical gown

Lights, Camera, Violence! The 2022 Academy Awards – Answers

1. B – Payne's appearance at the Oscars caused confusion on two fronts – firstly, his inexplicable 'Dutch-sounding' accent, and secondly the astonishing fact that Liam Payne is still famous enough to attend the Oscars.

2. C – Historically, heist movies have performed well at the Oscars, but shockingly this one, featuring former wrestler Dave Bautista and [checks notes] a zombie tiger, was sadly overlooked in the main categories.

3. A – First the pandemic, then the war in Ukraine and now 'woman spotted wearing shorts'? They do say things come in threes, and massive global news stories are no exception.

4. C – Unfortunately DiCaprio left before the joke was made, as his girlfriend had a maths test first thing Monday morning.

5. C – The ceremony included the 'Worst Performance by Bruce Willis in a 2021 Movie' category, which saw Bruce Willis go up against Bruce Willis, Bruce Willis and Bruce Willis. In case you're wondering, the win went to bookies' favourite Bruce Willis. Organisers did however rescind the category a week later when Willis retired from acting due to ill health.

6. B – *Diana: The Musical* picked up five Razzies in total, including the lucrative Worst Actor, Worst Film and Worst Director awards.

7. D – Specifically, he threatened to smelt them in public. Incredibly, the threat of a middle-aged man melting his own knick-knacks at the side of the road didn't sway the Academy and Zelenskyy didn't get to speak.

8. B – In an interview that Erwin Schrödinger would have been proud of, Radcliffe said he was 'dramatically bored' of hearing about Will Smith while simultaneously talking about Will Smith.

9. A – Smith issued a grovelling apology and resigned from the Academy, after Tommy Lee Jones refused to let him use the neuralyzer again.

10. C – Zimmer was in a hotel in Amsterdam when he gave an acceptance speech for the Academy Award for his work on sci-fi epic *Dune*. Fortunately the robe stayed in place, keeping his sandworm under wraps.

LONDON'S HOTTEST PARTY VENUE PART 2: ELECTRIC BOOGALOO

Just when it seemed people had forgotten about lock-down parties at No. 10 (on account of the marginally bigger story of Russa invading Ukraine) the Met issued their first round of fixed penalty notices, and we were back at square one.

1. On 12 April Boris Johnson and Rishi Sunak received £50 fixed penalty notices after being found to have breached Covid rules. In stark contrast, a woman from Peterlee was fined £10,000 for organising what?

    A. A balloon launch

    B. A charity walk

    C. A candlelight vigil

    D. A karaoke competition

2. Whenever partygate was in the news, a hare-brained quote from Michael Fabricant was sure to follow. In the days following Johnson and Sunak's fines, he angered teachers and nurses by suggesting they did what at the end of the day during lockdown?

    A. Removed masks

    B. Shared biscuits and magazines

    C. Drank alcohol

    D. Held quizzes

3. In his first Commons address after the fines were issued, Boris Johnson got off fairly lightly, being admonished by only one of his own MPs, but can you remember who it was?

    A. Steve Baker

    B. Mark Harper

    C. Sir Roger Gale

    D. Jeremy Hunt

4. As the tables turned on Labour amid mounting scrutiny over their own 'work event' in 2021, what type of curry did Tory backbencher Graham Stuart reference in an admittedly funny line aimed at Keir Starmer?

    A. Jalfrezi

    B. Madras

    C. Balti

    D. Korma

5. Not willing to let the story go, what did Boris Johnson say to Keir Starmer as they walked together ahead of the Queen's speech?

    A. 'Know any good lawyers?'

    B. 'Quiet weekend?'

    C. 'Fancy a swift one after work?'

    D. 'Don't fill up on poppadums.'

6. During an interview with Sophie Raworth on the
    BBC's *Sunday Morning* programme that inevitably
    kept returning to the issue of partygate, former Health
    Secretary Jeremy Hunt twice declined to say that
    Boris Johnson was what?

    A. Pressuring MPs to defend him
    B. Someone he considered a friend
    C. An honest man
    D. The best person for the job

7. When the Met finally concluded its investigation,
    what was the total number of fixed penalty notices
    issued in relation to Downing Street 'work events'?

    A. 56
    B. 96
    C. 126
    D. 156

8. A few days after the investigation ended, photos were
    obtained by ITV of Boris Johnson raising a glass
    during purported leaving drinks for which departing
    member of staff?

    A. Lee Cain
    B. Dominic Cummings
    C. Munira Mirza
    D. Dan Rosenfield

9. On 13 July Keir Starmer attended PMQs for the first time since being cleared of breaching lockdown rules, and Boris Johnson had saved his most ridiculous nickname for the Labour leader until last. What did he call him?

    A. Major General Hindsight

    B. Captain Dullard McSpineless

    C. Captain Crasharoonie Snoozefest

    D. Snoozemaster 3000

10. Upon clearing Keir Starmer and Angela Rayner of any wrongdoing, police described the curry and beer event as what?

    A. Reasonably necessary work

    B. A well-earned meal

    C. Justified sustenance

    D. A business luncheon

London's Hottest Party Venue Part 2:
Electric Boogaloo – Answers

1. A – Vicki Hutchinson from Peterlee organized the balloon launch in memory of her father-in-law and refused to pay the £10,000 fine, eventually having to pay £135 in costs instead, which was still nearly three times what the people who made the laws in the first place had to pay.

2. C – After outrage over his claims that teachers and nurses enjoyed 'a quiet drink' at the end of a long shift, Fabricant claimed that he never meant to cause offence, which can't be true or he'd only do radio interviews.

3. B – Former Tory chief whip and MP for Forest of Dean Mark Harper said he no longer deemed Johnson to be worthy of the office he holds. A confusing statement as it implies he once was.

4. D – Stuart said, 'Never in the history of human conflict has so much karma come from a korma.' Good delivery aside, the bland, inoffensive choice of the unadventurous is still hoping to defeat the government at the next election.

5. B – The PM enquired about Starmer's weekend plans ahead of the state opening of Parliament, although the joke's on him as all weekends are quiet when you're Keir Starmer.

6. C – When asked whether the PM is an honest man, Jeremy Hunt said 'talking about personalities is not a helpful thing to do', which to be fair is a sensible route to take if you don't have one.

7. C – As the old saying goes, fool me once, shame on you. Fool me 126 times, also shame on you, and throw some junior ministers under the bus while you're at it.

8. A – The photo from ex-communications director Lee Cain's leaving do appeared to show eight people and seven bottles of booze, although it's entirely plausible that the PM didn't notice them as the room wasn't particularly well lit and he was at least ten inches away.

9. C – Johnson called Starmer 'Captain Crasharoonie Snoozefest', which – love him or hate him – was admittedly quite funny from the outgoing PM.

10. A – Police described the event as 'reasonably necessary work', as Labour were clearly brainstorming many of the 0 policies they've announced in the two years since.

Oldest and Youngest Presidents

The twenty-first century has seen US presidents at both extremes of the age spectrum (with 2022 seeing an octogenarian in the Oval Office for the first time). But can you work out the five oldest and youngest* commanders-in-chief from the clues below?

(* Ages as of the date they assumed office)

Oldest

1. *(78 years, 61 days)* Was sworn in as the US's oldest president amid heightened security due to his opponent disputing the election result and the small matter of a recent armed insurrection at the Capitol Building.
2. *(70 years, 220 days)* A self-professed 'stable genius', he became the first sitting US president to step into North Korea. Conducted much of his work remotely, usually from the back nine.
3. *(69 years, 349 days)* Served two terms in the White House after swapping Hollywood for Washington. Won one of the most lopsided election victories in US history after securing 525 of the 538 electoral college votes.
4. *(68 years, 23 days)* Holder of several unwanted records, including shortest presidency in US history (thirty-one days) and the first president to die in office. Notable achievements as president include being inaugurated and rearranging a few items of furniture in the White House.
5. *(65 years, 315 days)* Constantly ranked as one of the US's worst presidents by scholars and historians due to indecisiveness on the issue of slavery in the lead-up to the civil war. The only US president to not get married.

Youngest

1. *(42 years, 322 days)* Became the youngest US president of all time after his predecessor was assassinated. Polls often rank him as one of the greatest US presidents due to his progressive policies, and he won the Nobel Peace Prize for his role in ending the Russo-Japanese war.

2. *(43 years, 236 days)* The youngest elected president in US history, and sadly the one with the shortest lifespan. A popular urban legend (which has since been debunked) claims he declared himself to be a doughnut while visiting Berlin.

3. *(46 years, 154 days)* Served two terms, although his second was dominated by a sex scandal which led to him becoming one of only three presidents to be impeached. A keen saxophonist, and the first US president to visit Northern Ireland.

4. *(46 years, 311 days)* The US president with arguably the funniest name, he was a military man whose war hero image resonated well with voters. Was instrumental in the creation of the Justice Department, which in turn was key to the collapse of the Ku Klux Klan.

5. *(47 years, 169 days)* Born in Hawaii (or Kenya, according to people in YouTube comment sections), he served two terms and was the first sitting US president to visit Hiroshima and to address both houses of the UK Parliament. Also a two-time Grammy winner in the Best Spoken Word Album category.

Oldest and Youngest Presidents – Answers

Oldest

1. Joe Biden
2. Donald J. Trump
3. Ronald Reagan
4. William Henry Harrison
5. James Buchanan

Youngest

1. Theodore Roosevelt
2. John F. Kennedy
3. Bill Clinton
4. Ulysses S. Grant
5. Barack Obama

2022 GENERAL KNOWLEDGE – ROUND 3

Here's the third of our four general knowledge rounds of the year. Good luck!

1. In August, Leeds County Council ruled that a 150-year-old local landmark had to be shortened by six metres on health and safety grounds after a long battle with campaigners seeking to preserve it. What was the landmark?

    A. A church spire
    B. A chimney
    C. A statue of Aristotle
    D. An oak tree

2. Andy Murray exited Wimbledon 2022 after losing in the second round to American John Isner. What record did Isner's match against Nicolas Mahut break at Wimbledon 2010?

    A. Most games played while snowing
    B. Quickest men's match in history
    C. Longest tennis match in history
    D. It had three different umpires

3. On 15 July Joe Biden was strongly criticised after fist-bumping which other world leader?

    A. Xi Jinping

    B. Alexander Lukashenko

    C. Jair Bolsonaro

    D. Mohammed bin Salman

4. During a summer trip to Italy with his family, actor Russell Crowe found himself in hot water after doing what inside the Sistine Chapel?

    A. Taking off his shoes

    B. Shouting at a tour guide

    C. Taking photographs

    D. Vaping

5. As Covid cases began rising sharply in March, what detailed scientific advice did then-Health Secretary Sajid Javid give?

    A. 'Brace for it'

    B. 'Use common sense'

    C. 'Be careful'

    D. 'Don't do anything I wouldn't do'

6. Long-running Australian soap *Neighbours* ended in 2022 after thirty-seven years on our screens. Which of the following actors didn't appear in the final episode?

    A. Kylie Minogue

    B. Margot Robbie

    C. Isla Fisher

    D. Natalie Imbruglia

7. Former mayor of New York/loyal Donald Trump associate Rudy Giuliani tried his hand at being a social media influencer in late June when he promoted what on Twitter?

    A. Hearing aids

    B. Sandals

    C. Moisturiser

    D. Cryptocurrency

8. When York City Council told binman Lee Moran that he couldn't wear shorts on health and safety grounds, what did he wear instead?

    A. A tuxedo

    B. Hotpants

    C. Leggings

    D. A kilt

9. During the record-breaking heatwave in July, which Christmas film did Channel 4 broadcast as temperatures hit 40°C?

   A. *It's a Wonderful Life*
   B. *White Christmas*
   C. *Home Alone*
   D. *The Polar Express*

10. In one of the year's stranger marketing ploys, Deliveroo released a dance track that the company claimed prevented what?

   A. Seagulls stealing chips
   B. Food going cold
   C. The meat sweats
   D. People putting on weight

2022 General Knowledge – Round 3 Answers

1. B – It was a chimney. Campaigners had long been at odds with Leeds County Council over the potential removal of the Victorian chimney at Stonebridge Mills in Farnley, but reluctantly accepted that it would need to be shortened. Jacob Rees-Mogg also welcomed the move, as it will take far less time for children to clean it.

2. C – It was the longest tennis match of all time (by quite some distance). Isner and Mahut's first-round tie at the 2010 championships lasted eleven hours and five minutes over three days, with the final set alone (70–68) lasting longer than the previous longest match. The record will never be beaten as a rule was later introduced to force a tie-break in cases where the fifth set reaches 12–12.

3. D – Despite publicly condemning Mohammed bin Salman over alleged ties to the killing of journalist Jamal Khashoggi, seventy-nine-year-old Biden shared a friendly fist-bump with the Saudi crown prince during a trip to Jeddah in July. White House officials said Biden fist-bumped bin Salman for health reasons – perhaps he didn't want to catch mass murder from him.

4. C – Russell Crowe was criticised for taking photo-graphs inside the Sistine Chapel, but Australians (and New Zealanders, for the pedants among you) argued that he should be let off as a gesture of goodwill since Rome wasn't really known for anything until *Gladiator* came out.

5. A – At a time when an estimated one in twenty-five people in England were thought to have Covid, the Health Secretary advised everyone to brace for it, before spinning on his heel and walking off into the sunset. Then again, still clearer than 'hands, face, space'.

6. C – Isla Fisher didn't appear in the finale because she was never in *Neighbours*, but rather rival soap *Home and Away*. As well as Kylie Minogue, Margot Robbie, Natalie Imbruglia and Delta Goodrem, the finale also featured a bit of eye candy for the ladies in the shape of Harold Bishop.

7. B – Giuliani posted a tweet promoting discount sandals, and – not for the first time – found himself the laughing stock of Twitter. It doesn't appear he saw the funny side though, as he immediately blocked *Have I Got News for You* for highlighting the absurdity of the whole thing.

8. D – A high-vis kilt to be precise, which the fifty-year-old binman says has been really well received by the public (and to answer the question you're all wondering, we're not sure as he hasn't been out on a windy day yet).

9. B – As the UK sweltered in record-breaking heat on 18 July, *White Christmas* was shown on Film4, although we can kiss goodbye to ironic wackiness like this if the government succeeds in making Channel 4 pay for occasionally saying mean things about them.

10. A – Deliveroo released a song which apparently prevents chips being stolen while at the beach. Hopefully seagulls will go after workers' rights next so the company might protect those as well.

THE UGLY GAME

A lot happened in the world of football in 2022. Liverpool came agonisingly (or hilariously, depending on your standpoint) close to an historic quadruple, Nottingham Forest returned to the Premier League after twenty-three years, the Lionesses did what the men's team couldn't by winning the Euros, and of course there's the small matter of the Qatar World Cup (if you're wondering why there are no questions about it, it's because we had far more interesting questions to include, and not because the tournament kicked off after we went to print) so try your ~~hand~~ foot at these ten questions (points to be deducted if you go into administration).

1. In 2022, which football club became the first to have beaten all the other ninety-one teams in the English top four divisions, a stat 130 years in the making?

    A. Accrington Stanley
    B. Wolverhampton Wanderers
    C. Derby County
    D. Port Vale

2. In February, Harry Kane and Son Heung-min became the Premier League's all-time highest-scoring partnership – combining for (at that point) thirty-seven goals – but which duo previously held the record?

    A. Frank Lampard and Didier Drogba
    B. Sergio Agüero and David Silva
    C. Chris Sutton and Alan Shearer
    D. Teddy Sheringham and Darren Anderton

3. Which World Cup-winning football legend turned out for a Shropshire pub side in March, scoring in the process?

    A. Zinedine Zidane
    B. Alessandro Del Piero
    C. Roberto Carlos
    D. Miroslav Klose

4. Liverpool beat Chelsea 11–10 on penalties in the 2022 League Cup final, with Kepa Arrizabalaga missing the deciding spot kick – but what did he do in the 2019 final to make the miss especially satisfying?

    A. He got sent off
    B. He verbally abused a ball boy
    C. He refused to be subbed off
    D. He broke the trophy

5. Which of the following teams didn't get promoted at the end of the 2021/22 season?

    A. Exeter City
    B. Wigan Athletic
    C. Scunthorpe United
    D. Forest Green Rovers

6. During a football match in Jamaica on 23 March, Raheem Sterling scored after an assist from which unlikely source?

    A. Usain Bolt
    B. Prince William
    C. Shaggy
    D. Pelé

7. After the Lionesses' historic Euros victory at Wembley, why did match-winner Chloe Kelly suddenly run away during a pitch-side interview?

    A. She spotted a family member
    B. To join a team photo
    C. Neil Diamond was playing
    D. She was attacked by a wasp

8. Chloe Kelly also made headlines for her choice of celebration upon scoring the winning goal. What did she do?

    A. A backflip
    B. The robot
    C. Removed her shirt
    D. A Ronaldo-style 'SIUUUU!'

9. At the 2021 African Cup of Nations (which was delayed until 2022 due to the pandemic), which team – ranked 132nd in the world – caused a shock upset by knocking out four-time AFCON champions Ghana?

    A. Comoros
    B. Burkina Faso
    C. Malawi
    D. Gabon

10. Manchester City strengthened their already imposing squad by signing Norwegian striker Erling Haaland for £51.2 million. What incredible feat did he achieve in a game against Honduras at the 2019 U20 World Cup?

    A. He scored two scorpion kicks
    B. He received the first ever 10.0 rating
    C. He scored a triple hat trick
    D. He broke the crossbar

The Ugly Game – Answers

1. D – The Valiants achieved what will surely go on to be one of the all-time great pub quiz questions after beating Sutton United on 26 March, meaning they'd beaten every other team currently in the top four divisions over the course of 130 years.

2. A – Chelsea legends Lampard and Drogba were the previous holders, combining for thirty-six goals. Teddy Sheringham and Darren Anderton are fifth on the list with twenty-seven goals, which for Darren Anderton, works out to about twenty-seven goals per game played.

3. C – Bull In The Barne FC won the services of the Brazil legend via a charity eBay auction, where he'd presumably been playing in the reserves. (Ahem, sorry.)

4. C – In the 2019 final against Manchester City, Arrizabalaga refused to be substituted at the end of extra time, before losing that penalty shootout as well. Chelsea also reached this year's FA Cup final and opted for Édouard Mendy in goal instead, comfortably beating Liver— just kidding, they lost on penalties again.

5. C – It was Scunthorpe, who not only didn't get promoted, but were relegated from the football league altogether after seventy-two years following a 3–0 defeat to Leyton Orient.

6. B – It was Prince William, during his ill-fated tour of the Caribbean. Playing with the Man City forward was particularly confusing for the future king, as usually Sterling has his nan's face slapped on the side of it.

7. C – The interview abruptly ended when Chloe Kelly sprinted off to sing Neil Diamond's 'Sweet Caroline' with her teammates (although she did return a few minutes later). After their historic win, the FA was quick to offer congratulations to the Lionesses, and pledged to increase funding for women's football from £3.50 to just over a tenner.

8. C – She removed her shirt. The celebration was seen as a huge step in bringing women's football in line with the men's game – soon to follow: diving, blatant time-wasting and pathetically rolling around in agony.

9. A – In addition to reaching the knockout stage, Comoros also provided the holy grail of televised football: an outfield player in goal. Covid cases and injuries forced left-back Chaker Alhadhur to play their round-of-sixteen match against Cameroon between the sticks. Despite this – and playing for eighty minutes with ten men after an early red card – the Coelacanths only narrowly lost 2–1 to Cameroon. Fair play.

10. C – Not only did Haaland score an unprecedented triple hat trick, but incredibly he won the tournament's golden boot despite not scoring in any other game (Norway didn't even get out of the group stage).

BARGAIN BIN BOX OFFICE

Can you work out the A-list actors who made headlines in 2022 from a selection of their film credits?

1. Urban Legend *(1998)*, Panic Room *(2002)*, Alexander *(2004)*, Suicide Squad *(2016)*, House of Gucci *(2021)*.

    A. Matt Damon
    B. Joaquin Phoenix
    C. Chris Hemsworth
    D. Jared Leto

2. The Tale of Despereux *(2008)*, The Perks of Being a Wallflower *(2012)*, This Is the End *(2013)*, The Colony *(2015)*, The Circle *(2017)*.

    A. Eddie Redmayne
    B. Emma Watson
    C. Rupert Grint
    D. Emily Blunt

3. Where the Day Takes You *(1992)*, Six Degrees of Separation *(1993)*, The Legend of Bagger Vance *(2000)*, After Earth *(2013)*, Bright *(2017)*.

    A. Matt Damon
    B. Courtney Cox
    C. Will Smith
    D. Anne Hathaway

4. A Nightmare on Elm Street *(1984)*, What's Eating Gilbert Grape *(1993)*, The Ninth Gate *(1999)*, The Lone Ranger *(2013)*, Mortdecai *(2015)*.

   A. Johnny Depp
   B. Benedict Cumberbatch
   C. Tom Hiddleston
   D. Hugh Jackman

5. All the Boys Love Mandy Lane *(2006)*, Pineapple Express *(2008)*, Zombieland *(2009)*, Magic Mike XXL *(2015)*, Aquaman *(2018)*.

   A. Gal Gadot
   B. Reese Witherspoon
   C. Kate Winslet
   D. Amber Heard

6. Critters 3 *(1991)*, The Basketball Diaries *(1995)*, The Man in the Iron Mask *(1998)*, Body of Lies *(2008)*, J. Edgar *(2011)*.

   A. Mel Gibson
   B. Leonardo DiCaprio
   C. Mickey Rourke
   D. Danny Glover

7. The Color Purple *(1985)*, Ghost *(1990)*, How Stella Got Her Groove Back *(1998)*, Girl, Interrupted *(1999)*, Teenage Mutant Ninja Turtles *(2014)*.

   A. Melissa McCarthy
   B. Whoopi Goldberg
   C. Glenn Close
   D. Queen Latifah

8. Raising Arizona *(1987)*, Snake Eyes *(1998)*, Lord of War *(2005)*, Season of the Witch *(2011)*, Willy's Wonderland *(2021)*.

   A. Vin Diesel
   B. Jason Statham
   C. Nicolas Cage
   D. John Travolta

9. American Gangster *(2007)*, RocknRolla *(2008)*, Ghost Rider: Spirit of Vengeance *(2011)*, The Dark Tower *(2017)*, Cats *(2019)*.

   A. Idris Elba
   B. Dwayne Johnson
   C. Gerard Butler
   D. Denzel Washington

10. Much Ado About Nothing *(1993)*, Wild Wild West *(1999)*, Five Children and It *(2004)*, Jack Ryan: Shadow Recruit *(2014)*, Death on the Nile *(2022)*.

    A. Kenneth Branagh

    B. Colin Firth

    C. Sean Bean

    D. Jim Broadbent

Bargain Bin Box Office Answers

1. D – **Jared Leto** – His notorious method acting caused debate in 2022 when director Daniel Espinosa revealed Leto used a wheelchair to travel to and from the bathroom on the set of *Morbius*, despite not needing one in real life.

2. B – **Emma Watson** – The *Harry Potter* actress found herself in the middle of an antisemitism storm in January after posting a pro-Palestine image on social media, leading to an open letter of support from more than forty celebrities, including Mark Ruffalo, Susan Sarandon and Steve Coogan.

3. C – **Will Smith** – Won an Oscar for his portrayal of Richard Williams, but otherwise steered clear of drama and had a fairly quiet year.

4. A – **Johnny Depp** – Spent the early part of the year in a messy court battle with . . .

5. D – **Amber Heard** – The pair attempted to sue one another, and the result was messier and harder to watch than any of their films (yes, even *Salazar's Revenge*).

6. B – **Leonardo DiCaprio** – In March news outlets around the world were fooled into sharing reports that the star had donated $10 million to Ukraine because his grandmother was born there, despite both claims being debunked days later.

7. B – **Whoopi Goldberg** – The US actress made headlines for all the wrong reasons after being suspended from daytime show *The View* after claiming the Holocaust 'isn't about race'.

8. C – **Nicolas Cage** – Followed in the footsteps of John Malkovich and Bill Murray by playing himself in a film (*The Unbearable Weight of Massive Talent*) which, perhaps surprisingly, was fairly well received and a commercial success.

9. A – **Idris Elba** – The veteran British actor teamed up with the BBC to help young people transform their lives through boxing, and, in one of his stranger film roles, voiced Knuckles the Echidna in *Sonic the Hedgehog 2*.

10. A – **Kenneth Branagh** – After thirty-two years and eight nominations, Branagh finally won an Oscar in 2022, picking up Best Original Screenplay for *Belfast*.

MISSING WORDS – ROUND 3

More incomplete headlines to complete at your leisure . . .

1. House with _____ sticking out of roof given
   listed building status despite owner's objections
   Independent – 25 March

   A. First World War bomb
   B. Giant shark
   C. Obscene chimney
   D. 1950s convertible

2. Is Putin going to have to stop _____ because
   of sanctions on Russia?
   Independent – 18 March

   A. Horse-riding
   B. Using Botox
   C. Going out in public
   D. Scrapbooking

3. Religious artwork removed after _____ found
   among holy images
   Sky News – 15 February

   A. Characters from *Austin Powers*
   B. Church window cleaner
   C. Local priest and businessman
   D. Barry from *EastEnders*

4. Man slammed for asking sister to pay for his wedding, then _____
   Mirror – 20 March

   A. Cancelling it
   B. Not turning up
   C. Uninviting her
   D. Upgrading the venue

5. Statue of saint that looks like _____ distracts homebuyers in Dorset town
   Dorset Live – 21 March

   A. A giant owl
   B. Nicolas Cage
   C. The Jolly Green Giant
   D. Bob Marley

6. I have a _____ living in my house – guests hate it but I won't kill it
   Mirror – 22 March

   A. Venomous scorpion
   B. Three-foot lizard
   C. Feral pig
   D. Huge spider

7. I let a baby bird nest in my _____ for 84 days
   Guardian – 25 March

   A. Bed
   B. Hair
   C. Boyfriend's car
   D. Grandmother's urn

8. Is _____ TV's successor to David Attenborough? Netflix is banking on it
   Tech Radar – 16 March

   A. Barack Obama
   B. Prince Harry
   C. Marie Kondo
   D. Jonathan van Ness

9. Woman mortified as chicken shop 'free sample' turns out to be _____
   Mirror – 25 March

   A. Dead pigeon
   B. Three days old
   C. Stranger's order
   D. Made of plastic

264

10. Football club accidentally names stand after

_____

The Week – 4 August

A. Pol Pot

B. Rose West

C. Harold Shipman

D. Osama bin Laden

MISSING WORDS – ROUND 3 ANSWERS

1. **B** – 'House with **giant shark** sticking out of roof given listed building status despite owner's objections.' The twenty-five-foot 'Headington Shark' was installed in the 1980s by artist Bill Heine and has protruded from the roof of the house ever since. Just when you thought it was safe to go back in the loft . . .

2. **B** – 'Is Putin going to have to stop **using Botox** because of sanctions on Russia?' The Russian president reportedly hates allegations that he uses Botox, and desperately attempts to frown whenever someone brings it up.

3. **C** – 'Religious artwork removed after **local priest and businessman** found among holy images.' Eagle-eyed churchgoers spotted the pair in the painting gifted to a church in Southern Italy, although have yet to find Wally, Wanda or Wizard Whitebeard.

4. **C** – 'Man slammed for asking sister to pay for his wedding, then **uninviting her**.' The siblings' mum decided that the best place to seek advice on this sensitive family issue was Reddit, which is like trying to cure a nut allergy by swimming in Sun-Pat.

5. **B** – 'Statue of saint that looks like **Nicolas Cage** distracts homebuyers in Dorset town.' A house-hunter in Poole was shocked to discover the six-foot statue in the corner of an otherwise empty house. Similarities between the statue and Nic Cage included facial features, height, and being completely wooden.

6. **D** – 'I have a **huge spider** living in my house – guests hate it but I won't kill it.' A twenty-six-year-old woman revealed that she'd named the giant huntsman spider Simon and lets him wander around her house at will. Three guesses as to where she … It's Australia. Of course it's Australia.

7. **B** – 'I let a baby bird nest in my **hair** for 84 days.' A photographer living in Ghana revealed how she raised the bird for nearly three months by letting it live in her hair. Brings a whole new meaning to Dove 2 in 1.

8. **A** – 'Is **Barack Obama** TV's successor to David Attenborough?' Netflix is banking on it. After the butter-wouldn't-melt former US president drew the comparison by narrating a nature series about wildlife, Sir David repaid the compliment with a series of botched drone strikes.

9. **C** – 'Woman mortified as chicken shop 'free sample' turns out to be **stranger's order**.' An embarrassing faux pas, sure, but surprisingly few people pointed out the many, many alarm bells that should have been set off by 'free samples outside chicken takeaway' in the first place.

10. **B** – 'Football club accidentally names stand after **Rose West**.' Southend United secured a sponsorship deal with local estate agent Gilbert & Rose over the summer, which included naming rights over their west stand. Unfortunately the Gilbert & Rose West Stand only lasted a couple of days before the club realised the mistake and struck a new sponsorship deal with local builder Edward Bundy.

BETWEEN THE DEVIL AND THE DEEP BROWN SEA

Holidaying in the UK was a great idea in 2022 as long as you didn't fancy a dip in the sea, as heavy rainfall caused large swathes of it to be replaced by sewage overflow. The following English coastal towns and cities were all affected, but can you place them on a map?

1. Morecambe
2. Southend
3. Worthing
4. Cleethorpes
5. Eastbourne
6. Falmouth
7. Redcar
8. Minehead
9. Folkestone
10. Exmouth

Between the Devil and the Deep Brown Sea – Answers

NAME THAT CBEEBIES SHOW

In 2022 it was announced that CBeebies is to be discontinued as a broadcast TV channel and will transition to digital over the next few years. Since launching in 2002 it has featured countless adorable (and sometimes horrifying) shows and characters. How many of the following can you work out from the descriptions below?

1. Manual labourer who gets around staffing costs by using sentient tools and vehicles. Voiced by Neil Morrissey, the show achieved two UK number one singles.

   A. *Bitz & Bob*
   B. *Driver Dan's Story Train*
   C. *Bob the Builder*
   D. *Mister Maker*

2. Derek Jacobi narrates as Igglepiggle, Makka Pakka, Upsy Daisy and the Tombliboos agonise over whether to ride the Ninky Nonk or the Pinky Ponk. Culminates when the Tittifers decide it's time for everyone to go to sleep.

   A. *Higgledy House*
   B. *Doodle Do*
   C. *Tots TV*
   D. *In the Night Garden*

3. Started out as a feature on the CBeebies website
   but proved so popular that it got its own series.
   Sort of like a pre-school *Thunderbirds*, with
   characters Xuli, Kyan, Lars, Foz and Ubercorn
   travelling the world in their signature vehicles,
   solving mysteries, and battling evil supervillain
   Grandmaster Glitch.

   A. *Go Jetters*
   B. *The Octonauts*
   C. *Kazoops!*
   D. *Kerwhizz*

4. Filmed in the Yorkshire seaside town of Staithes, this
   show starred *Doctor Who* alumni Bernard Cribbins
   and Freema Agyeman.

   A. *Old Jack's Boat*
   B. *Something Special*
   C. *Grandpa in My Pocket*
   D. *Apple Tree House*

5. Follows the exploits of a worryingly clumsy man, his obedient robot servant Robert, and their friends Little Monster, Cousin Cuddle and Auntie Monsterella. Features one of the catchiest theme songs on the list, or most annoying if you're over the age of four.

    A. *Balamory*

    B. *Something Special*

    C. *Justin's House*

    D. *Buzz and Tell*

6. Centred around an anthropomorphic rabbit and his favourite toy, Hoppity Voosh. He is looked after by a weird orange thing called Flop, who was voiced until 2015 by Mark Rylance.

    A. *Tinpo*

    B. *Bing*

    C. *Katie Morag*

    D. *Gigglebiz*

7. Based on a series of best-selling children's books created by Gareth and Jean Adamson in the 1960s. Tells the story of a pair of twins and their many adventures. Was initially released as a cartoon before receiving a live-action reboot in 2013.

    A. *Topsy and Tim*

    B. *Kiri and Lou*

    C. *Tee and Mo*

    D. *Woolly and Tig*

8. This one is firmly in the 'stuff of nightmares'
   category. It's aimed at pre-schoolers and features
   five multi-coloured monstrosities called Great
   BigHoo, Toodloo, Chickedy, Chick
   and Peekaboo.

   A. *Dipdap*

   B. *64 Zoo Lane*

   C. *Twirlywoos*

   D. *Bobinogs*

9. Follows an intrepid crimefighter and his band Da
   Easy Crew, who are repeatedly torn away from their
   musical exploits by the absolutely useless President
   Wensley Dale. Characters include Scratchy, Zoomer,
   Bandulu and Natty Kass. Features the voice talents
   of former *Top of the Pops* presenter and Radio One DJ
   Reggie Yates.

   A. *Rastamouse*

   B. *Yoho Ahoy*

   C. *Dr Otter*

   D. *Big Barn Farm*

10. Set on a monkey-shaped tropical island where everyone gets a little too excited about playing musical instruments. The show is centred around Zak, Tang, Panzee and Drum, who have children transported to their domain in a yellow submarine to sing and dance with them. Lasted only two years before being culled in 2012, just as the Mayans predicted.

    A.   *Rubbadubbers*

    B.   *Tweenies*

    C.   *Numberjacks*

    D.   *ZingZillas*

Name that CBeebies Show – Answers

1. **C** – *Bob the Builder*

2. **D** – *In the Night Garden*

3. **A** – *Go Jetters*

4. **A** – *Old Jack's Boat*

5. **C** – *Justin's House*

6. **B** – *Bing*

7. **A** – *Topsy and Tim*

8. **C** – *Twirlywoos*

9. **A** – *Rastamouse*

10. **D** – *ZingZillas*

Having fallen on hard times, the original Teletubbies followed ABBA's lead and appeared in public together for the first time since 2001 (minus Dipsy, who's serving eight years for GBH):

BIT NIPPY OUT: THE 2022 WEATHER AND CLIMATE ROUND

World leaders outdid themselves in in the fight against climate change in 2022 by shrugging up to 50 per cent more than previous years. These ten questions about weather and climate should kill five minutes while we wait for the end of days.

1. February was a bit on the draughty side, but which of the following storms did NOT batter the UK in 2022?

   A. Dudley
   B. Emma
   C. Eunice
   D. Franklin

2. On 18 February, a particularly windy day, live footage of what went viral, drawing more than 200,000 viewers?

   A. The UK's tallest tree
   B. Waves at Brighton beach
   C. The summit of Ben Nevis
   D. Planes landing at Heathrow

3. In March, Antarctica recorded temperatures of up to 40°C higher than usual. In response, what did Donald Trump claim that melting ice caps would create?

    A. More places to fish

    B. Tidal waves

    C. New cruise routes

    D. More homes by the ocean

4. In one of the year's more chilling (no pun intended) climate headlines, archaeologists announced that strong winds and increased rainfall were bringing what to the surface in southern Chile?

    A. Long-dormant viruses

    B. Ancient mummies

    C. Subterranean sand spiders

    D. Mole people

5. In 2022, companies stepped up efforts to create environmentally friendly products. A brewery in Singapore unveiled a beer made from what?

    A. Hydrogen

    B. Sea water

    C. Urine

    D. Bone marrow

6. A company in the US announced the construction of ten 250,000-litre vats which will be used to grow what?

    A. Milk

    B. Cheese

    C. Meat

    D. Manure

7. Why was Bristol mayor Marvin Rees criticised after giving a fourteen-minute speech on climate change?

    A. He flew nine hours to the event

    B. He swore forty-six times

    C. He denied that climate change is real

    D. People had paid £250 for tickets

8. Speaking at a Catholic event in Stuttgart, German chancellor Olaf Scholz sparked a backlash after he compared climate activists to what?

    A. Worms

    B. Parasites

    C. Nazis

    D. Neanderthals

9. Which famous artwork was targeted by a climate protester on 30 May?

    A. The *Mona Lisa*

    B. Michelangelo's *David*

    C. *Whistler's Mother*

    D. *Venus de Milo*

10. In another of the year's many climate protests, a woman tied herself to the net at the French Open and made which oddly specific claim?

    A. Net zero must be reached by 26 July

    B. The world will end in 2029

    C. 102 world leaders are to blame

    D. We have 1,028 days left

BIT NIPPY OUT: THE 2022 WEATHER AND CLIMATE ROUND – ANSWERS

1. B – Dudley, Eunice and Franklin hit the UK in quick succession between 16–21 February, whereas storm Emma arrived at the end of 2018's infamous Beast from the East, which made headlines after forcing several Newcastle fans to put their shirts back on.

2. D – Big Jet TV's livestream from Heathrow was required viewing, partly due to the anxiety-inducing footage of planes coming in sideways but mostly because of the sheer novelty of people going on holiday again post-Covid.

3. D – Rising sea levels would create more oceanfront real estate, according to everyone's favourite stable genius. No word on the homes that are already by the ocean though, like – oh, to pick one at random – Mar-a-Lago.

4. B – Chile's Chinchorro mummies have been preserved underground for 7,000 years, but are being exposed as extreme weather ravages the region. Scientists also say rising humidity is turning some of the bodies into a mysterious black goo, so there's a very good chance 'ancient mummy apocalypse' is on the cards for 2023.

5. C – It was claimed that urine-based beer could play a key part in fighting climate change, although bosses at Budweiser claimed they've been doing it for years.

6. C – It's claimed that up to 13,000 tonnes of synthetic meat will be grown inside colossal bioreactors, which will be closely monitored in order to avoid a turkey meltdown.

7. A – Rees made a 9,000-mile round trip to appear in person at the event in Canada. If only some sort of commonly used software existed that allowed people to communicate virtually then situations like this could be a thing of the past.

8. C – It was Nazis. Scholz was quick to defend the comparison, saying that there are actually 'very fine people' on both sides of the climate debate.

9. A – It was the *Mona Lisa*. According to eyewitnesses a man disguised as an elderly woman smeared cake on the bulletproof case that protects the famous painting before yelling 'think of the Earth'. When asked if it was a fruitcake, police said he was probably just a bit eccentric.

10. D – 1,028 days means the world is due to end on 28 March 2025, although if we really put our minds to it, we can probably get it out of the way before the next general election.

Badly Translated Quotes of 2022 – Round 2

Some more quotes from 2022 that have been butchered by Google Translate, but who said them?

1. 'I have seen a man and he standing on a stage and he make light of very serious. We did used to calling them jokes and do much laughing.'

   A. Sarah Millican

   B. Jimmy Carr

   C. Katherine Ryan

   D. Keith Lemon

2. 'Present on them side of my bed, was a human poop subject.'

   A. George Clooney

   B. Danny DeVito

   C. Johnny Depp

   D. Hugh Grant

3. 'Recently they banish them child scribe Joanne the Rowling because she – the author of an book that has gone hundred of million and million of copies . . . globe! fall out of favour with the being fans of them call it gender. freedom!'

    A. Marjorie Taylor Greene

    B. Marine Le Pen

    C. Donald Trump

    D. Vladimir Putin

4. 'I am very disappoint, I've having the nothing to say. Did something incredible happened tonight? yes we deserved to win €€€€ now we have been a great deal misfortune.'

    A. Gareth Southgate

    B. Roberto Mancini

    C. Gareth Bale

    D. Jürgen Klopp

5. 'Presently it is a time when the thing it is shifting. There will going to be a new order of the world outside of there, and we have got to being lead it. And, and we have got to being bringing together the rest of the free the world in doing the it.'

    A. Sir David Attenborough

    B. Jared Leto

    C. Joe Biden

    D. Xi Jinping

6. 'I loving my Eric dearly. I have know him since eternity and we have had ups and going downs. This Covid thing, it's splatted people up and make people sometimes go bananas for a while, do you know this?'

   A. Robert Plant
   B. Keith Richards
   C. Ringo Starr
   D. Ozzy Osbourne

7. 'I am would be wanting to see planet when we do begin to ultimate disband of all army friendships.'

   A. Jeremy Corbyn
   B. Diane Abbott
   C. Jess Phillips
   D. John McDonnell

8. 'I wanting to be an diplomat of that kind of the loving and care and worried. I would like to be to apologize to the Academy, I just wanting to do an apologize to all of my chosen.'

   A. Nicole Kidman
   B. Sean Penn
   C. Liza Minnelli
   D. Will Smith

9. 'We could even be supporting halt the battle under Toned Blair, at the time of the Iraq battle. So it is of the most interest yes that we can not be support of halt the battle now.'

    A.   David Lammy

    B.   Emily Thornberry

    C.   Lisa Nandy

    D.   Diane Abbott

10. 'He is the one who did oversaw this heinous big shenanigan at home and as well his office, he is the one that coming to them Parliament and said rules were complied with very, which clearly not case.'

    A.   Ed Davey

    B.   Keir Starmer

    C.   Nicola Sturgeon

    D.   Ian Blackford

Badly Translated Quotes – Round 2 Answers

1. B – 'You will say I saw a man and he stood on a stage and he made light of serious issues. We used to call them jokes and people would laugh.' – Jimmy Carr defending what was often referred to in the press as a Holocaust 'joke', despite the minor issue that no aspect of it was vaguely funny in any way.

Independent – 9 February

2. C – 'On my side of the bed was human faecal matter.' – Johnny Depp on the horrifying realisation that the mysterious object in his bed wasn't a melted Wonka bar.

Mirror – 20 April

3. D – 'Recently they cancelled the children's writer Joanne Rowling because she – the author of books that have sold hundreds of millions of copies worldwide – fell out of favour with fans of so-called gender freedoms.' – During a televised address Putin inexplicably likened his situation to that of J.K. Rowling. Definitely a Slytherin . . .

Guardian – 26 March

4. B – 'I'm more than disappointed, I've nothing to say. Something incredible happened tonight. We deserved to win the Euros, now we've been really unlucky.' – Italy manager Roberto Mancini after his side's shock (some might say hilarious) play-off loss to footballing giants North Macedonia.

talkSPORT – 25 March

5. C – 'Now is a time when things are shifting. There's going to be a new world order out there, and we've got to lead it. And we've got to unite the rest of the free world in doing it.' – Joe Biden sent conspiracy theorists into a frenzy by namedropping the fabled New World Order during a speech on Russia. The resulting spike in tinfoil-hat sales did however provide the US economy with a much-needed boost.

Evening Standard – 24 March

6. B – 'I love Eric dearly. I've known him since forever, and we've had ups and downs. This Covid thing, it's split people up and made people sometimes go awry for a while, you know?' – One of the world's leading experts on the effects of putting things in your body, Keith Richards shared his thoughts on Eric Clapton's views on Covid and vaccines.

NME – 19 March

7. A – 'I would want to see a world where we start to ultimately disband all military alliances.' – Jeremy Corbyn on NATO. Given the impact he had on the global stage as leader of the opposition, NATO unsurprisingly didn't pay much attention to the musings of an independent backbencher.

Daily Record – 20 April

8. D – 'I want to be an ambassador of that kind of love and care and concern. I want to apologize to the Academy, I want to apologize to all my fellow nominees.' – Will Smith apologising to the Academy for his unforgivable actions – namely slapping Chris Rock and appearing in *Wild Wild West*.

Digital Spy – 28 March

9. D – 'We could even support Stop the War under Tony Blair, at the time of the Iraq war. So it's interesting that we can't support Stop the War now.' – Diane Abbot, finding herself in the tragic position of looking back fondly at life under Tony Blair.

LabourList – 1 March

10. B – 'He is the one who oversaw this criminality at his home and his office, he is the one that came to Parliament and said all rules were complied with, which is clearly not the case.' – Keir Starmer as the first fixed penalty notices for Downing Street parties were issued, coming in at an unfathomably huge £50.

Guardian – 31 March

During a visit to the site of a new prison in Wrexham, there was a lengthy delay while Dominic Raab was freed from freshly poured concrete:

BIG DOG HAS FALLEN

After managing to keep his head above water for much of 2022, it all fell apart for Boris Johnson when Sajid Javid and Rishi Sunak resigned from the cabinet on 5 July, triggering a further fifty-seven resignations and eventually forcing the PM himself to throw in the towel. How much can you remember from the most exhausting forty-eight hours of the year?

1. After the many, many scandals that Boris Johnson survived during his premiership, the catalyst for his downfall was the appointment of which MP to the position of deputy chief whip?

   A. Steve Baker
   B. Chris Pincher
   C. William Wragg
   D. Crispin Blunt

2. Shortly after Sajid Javid and Rishi Sunak resigned, the government's trade envoy to Morocco, Andrew Murrison, took to Twitter to follow suit, but why was he widely ridiculed?

   A. Morocco's account replied with the 😂 emoji
   B. His resignation letter was illegible
   C. The letter was addressed to 'Borsi Johnson'
   D. He accidentally posted a selfie

3. As Boris Johnson rushed to replenish his cabinet after the initial resignations, which MP became the shortest-serving Education Secretary of all time?

   A. Lucy Allan

   B. Kemi Badenoch

   C. Karen Bradley

   D. Michelle Donelan

4. As the drama unfolded, what did Madame Tussauds Blackpool do with their Boris Johnson waxwork?

   A. Stood it outside the local Jobcentre

   B. Attached a sign saying 'ministers wanted'

   C. Sat it in the ticket office

   D. Moved it to the 'past leaders' display

5. One of the many government MPs who took to social media to announce that they'd withdrawn their support for Boris Johnson was Huw Merriman. What was notable about the timing of his tweet?

   A. He was sitting opposite Boris Johnson

   B. He'd pledged support ten minutes earlier

   C. He posted it at 2.30 a.m.

   D. He tweeted after the PM had already resigned

6. Eyebrows were raised when Piers Morgan introduced the 6 July edition of his ailing TalkTV show holding which animal?

    A. Cat
    B. Pig
    C. Snake
    D. Rat

7. As the BBC's Ros Atkins was reporting live from Downing Street with pressure increasing on the PM, what was news presenter Tim Willcox doing when the camera cut back to the studio?

    A. Eating a bowl of cereal
    B. Sitting with his feet on the desk
    C. A yoga pose
    D. Changing his shirt

8. As MPs tried to give interviews about the developing situation on Westminster's College Green, the Benny Hill theme was blasted from speakers, but which celebrity was responsible for the unwanted background music?

    A. Gary Lineker
    B. Sue Perkins
    C. Gary Neville
    D. Hugh Grant

9. When MP Andrea Jenkyns left Downing Street in the hours leading up to Boris Johnson's resignation, how did she react to the crowds gathered outside?

    A. She raised her middle finger

    B. She booed them

    C. She shouted 'shame!' twelve times

    D. She turned her back on them

10. On 8 July *The Times* featured a rundown of all the Tory MPs hoping to replace Boris Johnson, but why was the paper criticised over its choice of photo for Penny Mordaunt?

    A. She was wearing a swimming costume

    B. Her head had been cropped out

    C. She was holding three glasses of wine

    D. It wasn't Penny Mordaunt

Big Dog Has Fallen – Answers

1. B – It was Chris Pincher (whose name has a 'couldn't make it up' quality given that he was accused of drunkenly groping staff). The government's initial line was that Boris Johnson wasn't aware of any specific allegations against Pincher when he was appointed deputy chief whip, which – to the surprise of about three people nationwide – turned out to be untrue.

2. B – Andrew Murrison's resignation letter was illegible due to the lens on his camera being steamed up when he photographed it, leading some to claim that he'd sent the tweet from the bath. He posted a clearer version about twenty minutes later, which gave people – not least in Morocco – time to google who Andrew Murrison was.

3. D – MP for Chippenham Michele Donelan resigned as Education Secretary just two days after Boris Johnson appointed her. ITV reported that she was in line for £16,876.25 in severance pay, which must have been especially annoying for the PM, as that kind of money could have bought two rolls of wallpaper.

4. A – Madame Tussauds placed its Boris Johnson waxwork in front of Blackpool Jobcentre, causing a few double takes from passers-by. In truth, the waxwork wasn't particularly realistic, as it went the whole day without making any preposterous promises.

5. A – Huw Merriman was sat opposite Boris Johnson during the PM's Liaison Committee hearing when he hit send on the tweet, although what was already an embarrassing situation for the PM quickly became much worse as news broke that several ministers (including newly appointed Chancellor Nadhim Zahawi) were waiting for the PM at No. 10 to tell him to resign.

6. B – In an apparent reference to Boris Johnson's 'greased piglet' reputation, the controversial presenter introduced the show holding a live pig, which must have been a deeply unpleasant experience, and probably not very nice for Piers Morgan either.

7. B – As the camera cut back to the studio, presenter Tim Willcox was nonchalantly checking his phone with his feet up on the desk. He quickly regained his composure in the hope nobody noticed, and the clip was only viewed 6 million times on Twitter, so it looks like he got away with it.

8. D – Hugh Grant was to blame as MPs were drowned out by the *Benny Hill* theme while being interviewed about the latest developments from No. 10. The actor tweeted the suggestion to 'Stop Brexit Man' Steve Bray, who, not being one to shy away from attention of any kind, gleefully obliged.

9. A – Jenkyns raised her middle finger towards the waiting crowd, and was swiftly punished for her actions with a spot in Boris Johnson's makeshift cabinet.

10. A – She was wearing a swimming costume. Mordaunt took part in reality diving show *Splash!* in 2014, but the swimming costume photos were the least of her worries, as in typical Twitter fashion, footage of her spectacularly bellyflopping into the pool from ten metres quickly resurfaced and went viral. For some politicians (namely Boris Johnson), clumsily bellyflopping into a pool would have been PR gold, but Mordaunt would go on to fall at the last hurdle before sheepishly backing Liz Truss.

Odd One Out – Round 2

Four more things, but which is the odd one out and why?

1.

A: Laura Robson

B: Brendan Cole

C: Marine Le Pen

D: Sam Ryder

2.

A: Brooklyn Beckham

B: Rupert Murdoch

C: Britney Spears

D: Aziz Ansari

Odd One Out – Round 2 Answers

1. A – Laura Robson is the odd one out here. The other three were all runners-up in 2022 (Brendan Cole – *Dancing on Ice*, Marine Le Pen – the French presidential election, Sam Ryder – The Eurovision Song Contest) whereas Robson gave up: she announced her retirement in May, having not played competitively since 2019.

2. B – Rupert Murdoch doesn't belong here. Brooklyn Beckham, Britney Spears and Aziz Ansari all got married in 2022, whereas Murdoch's wife Jerry Hall filed for divorce in July. What attracted Jerry Hall to the billionaire media mogul in the first place is a complete mystery, other than the fact that he's very, very handsome.

There was a silver lining to the astronomical rise in petrol prices in 2022 as James Corden realised Carpool Karaoke was no longer viable:

MISSING WORDS – ROUND 4

1. 'Best ever' photo of _____ emerges 50 years after it was taken by a map maker
   Mirror – 8 May

   A. Bigfoot
   B. UFO
   C. Ghost
   D. Sea monster

2. _____ fans say childhood is 'ruined' after discovering what he looks like now
   Birmingham Mail – 9 May

   A. Basil Brush
   B. Mr Blobby
   C. Bob the Builder
   D. Charlie Chalk

3. Michael Gove tells people to 'calm down' _____ in bizarre interview
   Independent – 11 May

   A. Fourteen times
   B. In Latin
   C. About the cost of fuel
   D. In Scouse accent

4. Woman _____ during Metallica show as band play 'Enter Sandman'
   NME – 10 May

    A.   Marries husband
    B.   Hit by meteorite
    C.   Gives birth
    D.   Arrested for murder

5. Neighbour confuses _____ for elderly man unwell in the street
   Metro – 3 May 2022

    A.   Old trampoline
    B.   Pile of newspapers
    C.   Stack of traffic cones
    D.   Cardboard cut-out of Ant and Dec

6. Arby's manager caught on camera _____,
   police say
   NBC Chicago – 16 May

    A.   Punching man dressed as Elvis
    B.   Stealing customers' wallets
    C.   Having sex with a cheeseburger
    D.   Urinating in milkshake mix

7. Man stumbles across ' _____ ' stretching from ground in chilling discovery
    Mirror – 9 May

    A. Frozen horse
    B. Dead man's fingers
    C. Badger penis
    D. Human leg

8. Man spots _____ wrapped around his wing mirror while driving at 70mph on motorway
    Metro – 20 April

    A. £5,000 necklace
    B. Snake
    C. Wasp nest
    D. Six-week-old kitten

9. Woman rescued by firefighters after _____ trying to retrieve phone
    Evening Standard – 23 April

    A. Getting her head stuck in railings
    B. Driving off a cliff
    C. Climbing up a tree
    D. Falling into toilet

10. Adorable dog with '_____' is desperately searching for a new home
    Mirror – 16 May

    A. Ability to talk to humans

    B. Four left legs

    C. Receding hairline

    D. Famous parents

MISSING WORDS – ROUND 4 ANSWERS

1. B – '"Best ever" photo of **UFO** emerges 50 years after it was taken by a map maker.' The stunning image – captured in 1971 – shows a metallic disc flying over Costa Rica, and was the 238th most scrutinised photo of the year after the equally thrilling ones of Boris Johnson standing around eating cake.

2. C – '**Bob the Builder** fans say childhood is "ruined" after discovering what he looks like now.' As is the case with most classic kids' shows, Bob the Builder underwent a CGI revamp in 2022, and spent twenty-one of the twenty-four new episodes filling out paperwork for EU labourers.

3. D – 'Michael Gove tells people to "calm down" **in Scouse accent** in bizarre interview.' He also did a fairly convincing American accent during the appearance on *BBC Breakfast* in May, and the impressions didn't end there, as he spent the rest of the year pretending to be able to stand up straight near the Speaker's Chair.

4. C – 'Woman **gives birth** during Metallica show as band play "Enter Sandman".' Joice Figueiró went into labour during the band's encore and gave birth in the stadium's medical centre. Early reports suggested she'd had a C-section, but that's just where her seat was.

5. A – 'Neighbour confuses **old trampoline** for elderly man unwell in the street.' A man in Sunderland went over to check on what looked like an old man propped up against a wall only to find it was an old trampoline. He admits he should have realised when children started jumping up and down on it, but it's Sunderland so you can never be too sure.

6. D – 'Arby's manager caught on camera **urinating in milkshake mix**, police say.' The twenty-nine-year-old man in Washington state was recorded urinating into a bag of milkshake mix that may have been served to 'dozens of people'. Police say fortunately cases like this are extremely rare, as they require a working milkshake machine.

7. B – 'Man Stumbles across **"dead man's fingers"** stretching from ground in chilling discovery.' Not quite as gruesome as it sounds, as they were actually five mushrooms in the shape of a human hand. Better the mix-up happens this way round as it's infinitely worse to find a pinkie in your portobellos.

8. B – 'Man spots **snake** wrapped around his wing mirror while driving at 70mph on motorway.' A family driving on the M5 in Staffordshire were stunned when they spotted the slithery stowaway, although there was also a sense of relief as they'd thought the rattling was coming from the engine.

9. D – 'Woman rescued by firefighters after **falling into toilet** trying to retrieve phone.' The woman, who (shockingly) chose to remain anonymous, fell into a vault toilet at the top of Mount Walker near Seattle after dropping her phone. Firefighters say it's not the worst job they've been called out to, but it was a firm number two.

10. C – 'Adorable dog with **"receding hairline"** is desperately searching for a new home.' Cross-breed Freya – currently living in Bosnia but looking for a UK home – has a perfectly symmetrical patch of dark fur on her head that makes her look like a middle-aged insurance broker from Kent.

NAME THAT MP – ROUND 2

Here are another five MPs to guess from their various roles and ministerial positions, although given how this year's gone, some of the Tory ones may have held several (hundred) more since the book went to print.

1. MP for Esher and Walton *(2010– present)*

    Parliamentary Under-Secretary of State for Civil Liberties and Human Rights *(2015–2016)*
    Minister of State for Courts and Justice *(2017–2018)*
    Minister of State for Housing and Planning *(2018)*
    Secretary of State for Exiting the European Union *(2018)*
    Foreign Secretary, First Secretary of State *(2019–2021)*
    Justice Secretary, Deputy Prime Minister *(2021–2022)*

2. MP for Hackney North and Stoke Newington *(1987– present)*

    Shadow Minister of State for Public Health *(2010–2013)*
    Shadow Secretary of State for International Development *(2015–2016)*
    Shadow Health Secretary *(2016)*
    Shadow Home Secretary *(2016–2020)*

3. MP for Bromsgrove *(2010– present)*

    Economic Secretary to the Treasury *(2012–2013)*
    Financial Secretary to the Treasury *(2013–2014)*
    Culture Secretary *(2014–2015)*
    Business Secretary *(2015–2016)*
    Housing Secretary *(2016–2018)*
    Home Secretary *(2018–2019)*
    Chancellor of the Exchequer *(2019–2020)*
    Health Secretary *(2021–2022)*

4. MP for South Staffordshire *(2010– present)*

    Chief Whip of the House of Commons and
    Parliamentary Secretary to the Treasury *(2016–2017)*
    Defence Secretary *(2017–2019)*
    Education Secretary *(2019–2021)*

5. MP for Stratford-on-Avon *(2010– present)*

    Parliamentary Under-Secretary of State for Children
    and Families *(2018–2019)*
    Parliamentary Under-Secretary of State for Business
    and Industry *(2019–2021)*
    Parliamentary Under-Secretary of State for Covid-19
    Vaccine Deployment *(2020–2021)*
    Education Secretary *(2021–2022)*
    Chancellor of the Exchequer *(2022)*
    Chancellor of the Duchy of Lancaster, Minister
    for Intergovernmental Relations and Minister for
    Equalities *(2022– present)*

Name that MP – Round 2 Answers

1. Dominic Raab

2. Diane Abbott

3. Sajid Javid

4. Gavin Williamson

5. Nadhim Zahawi

During a speech in early 2022, there were several complaints after Matt Hancock became a bit too descriptive about his infamous tryst with Gina Coladangelo:

SOCIALLY SPEAKING – ROUND 2

Ten more social media posts from 2022, but can you remember who said it?

1. I am expecting a strong turnout of Conservative MPs at Prime Minister's Questions today. Not only to demonstrate their strong support for #Boris (!!). BUT also to prove they are NOT the one told by the Chief Whip to stay at home. I'll be there! 😜

   A. David Davis
   B. Damian Green
   C. Michael Fabricant
   D. Gary Sambrook

2. I am who I am .... He is who he is .... We are what we are and that's that!!!! 🛡 Life is for living, life goes on, life is not perfect at all and you know what .... It's OUR life no one else's. God bless. 🛡

   A. Gemma Collins
   B. Coleen Rooney
   C. Kourtney Kardashian
   D. Rebekah Vardy

3. If @spotify doesn't immediately remove @joerogan, I will release new music onto the platform. #youwerebeautiful

    A. Vanilla Ice
    B. David Guetta
    C. Victoria Beckham
    D. James Blunt

4. I'm excited to announce that today I will be on the Pyramid Stage at Glastonbury 5.15pm. See you there! @glastonbury

    A. Jeremy Corbyn
    B. Michelle Obama
    C. Greta Thunberg
    D. Marcus Rashford

5. The priority of all governments should be to stop Russia/help Ukraine. However it doesn't mean we should take our focus off this government hiking taxes to a post WW2 high, the PM being under police investigation and forget he's compromised/up to his neck in it with the Russians!

    A. Keir Starmer
    B. John Bercow
    C. James O'Brien
    D. Gary Neville

6. I am watching the women football and notice that ALL the commentators are women. I also note when mens football is on there is a symobilic female comentator to cover the broadcasters arse. Should I complain there should me a male commentator in women's football

    A. Alan Sugar
    B. Jim Davidson
    C. Katie Hopkins
    D. Sarah Vine

7. For consistency, should it not be the team at the Met who are investigating covid breaches at Number 10 who investigate the alleged covid breaches by Sir Keir Starmer and his team.

    A. Nadhim Zahawi
    B. Andrew Bridgen
    C. James Cleverly
    D. Nadine Dorries

8. Fathers. I cannot even begin to describe how wonderful it is when your daughter gets married to someone you like. I am being very unmanly about this weekend. It was just sublime. I have never been happier.

    A. Piers Morgan
    B. Andrew Neil
    C. Kevin Bishop
    D. Jeremy Clarkson

9. Oh and the new MnS in Stevenage is outrageously
   good

   A. John Lydon
   B. Liam Gallagher
   C. Ozzy Osbourne
   D. Thom Yorke

10. Just stopped by a constituent on the embankment
    in Wellingborough. He was Labour but joined the
    Conservatives because of Boris. 'Boris got us through
    Brexit and Covid. Leave him alone and let him get on
    with the job' I reckon that gentleman speaks for most
    of my constituents.

    A. Bill Cash
    B. Peter Bone
    C. Penny Mordaunt
    D. Karen Bradley

Socially Speaking – Round 2 Answers

1. C – Michael Fabricant (Twitter – 18 May) had a tendency in 2022 to make every single government crisis even worse by sharing the thoughts bouncing around in his well-insulated head. In this now-deleted tweet, he appeared to be making light of a colleague who had been arrested on suspicion of sexual assault.

2. B – Colleen Rooney (Twitter – 10 February) here with one of the great literary works. Hidden meanings, metaphors, a layered tapestry of . . . Just kidding, haven't a clue.

3. D – James Blunt (Twitter – 29 January) with the ultimate threat. A week later Spotify quietly removed 113 episodes of *The Joe Rogan Experience*, which was surely a coincidence . . . right?

4. C – Greta Thunberg (Twitter – 25 June) made an appearance on the Pyramid Stage, because nothing says getting smashed at a music festival like a speech about carbon emissions.

5. D – Gary Neville (Twitter – 23 March) joined Marcus Rashford and Jack Monroe on the list of non-politicians holding the government to account more effectively than the opposition.

6. A – Alan Sugar (Twitter – 9 July) received more than 7,300 replies to this tweet, which was as offensive to women as it was to the English language.

7. B – Andrew Bridgen (Twitter – 9 May) suggesting that the Metropolitan Police investigate a possible crime in the famous London borough of . . . Durham.

8. D – Jeremy Clarkson (Instagram – 22 May) at a boozy wedding is unquestionably the most stressful situation for catering staff to find themselves in.

9. B – Liam Gallagher (Twitter – 30 May) taking a quick break from promoting his new album and winding up Liverpool fans to remind everyone that rock 'n' roll isn't dead.

10. B – Peter Bone (Twitter – 31 May) received more than 10,000 replies after tweeting about the alleged encounter, including two or three that appeared to believe it happened.

2022 IN NUMBERS

The following numbers all relate to something from 2022, but can you match them up?

1. 23

2. 62,296

3. 3,549

4. 60

5. 650,000

6. 40.3

7. 25

8. 8

9. 378

10. 21,100,000

A. The record-breaking temperature (in Celsius) recorded in Coningsby, Lincolnshire on 19 July – the hottest ever recorded in the UK.

B. The energy price cap (in pounds) that Ofgem announced would go into effect on 1 October.

C. Emma Raducanu's 2022 earnings (in US dollars) according to the *Forbes* Tennis Rich List, published in August.

D. The number of runs England chased down on the final day of the Test match against India on 5 July.

E. The number of years that David Trefgarne – the UK's longest-serving peer – has sat in the House of Lords as of 31 March 2022.

F. The number of times Keir Starmer was found to have breached the MPs' code of conduct in August for failing to register interests on time.

G. The number of documents marked TOP SECRET found at Mar-a-Lago by the FBI on 8 August.

H. The winning bid (in pounds) for Princess Diana's Ford Escort when it sold at auction in August.

I. The number of goals Mo Salah and Son Heung-min each scored on their way to sharing the 2021–22 Premier League Golden Boot in May.

J. The number of fans in attendance at *Clash at the Castle* – the first ever WWE pay-per-view event to be held in Wales – on 3 September.

2022 in Numbers – Answers

1. I – Salah and Son each scored twenty-three goals to share the Premier League Golden Boot. Harry Kane has also won it on three occasions, meaning Tottenham's trophy room now consists of four Golden Boots.

2. J – 62,296 wrestling fans crammed into Cardiff's Principality Stadium on 3 September for *Clash at the Castle*, the first WWE (formally WWF) stadium pay-per-view to be held in the UK since SummerSlam '92. The crowd consisted of twenty children and 62,276 men who work in IT and still live with their mums.

3. B – Ofgem confirmed that the UK's energy price cap (which definitely exists) would rise to £3,549 on 1 October. One person whose home heating bills didn't go up however was Boris Johnson, as he simply spent the rest of the year on holiday.

4. E – David Trefgarne, 2nd Baron Trefgarne has sat in the House of Lords for sixty years, having first taken his seat on his twenty-first birthday in 1962. He spent a year as a trade minister under Margaret Thatcher but has otherwise spent his entire adult life struggling to stay awake on a red seat.

5. H – Princess Di's 1985 Ford Escort sold for £650,000 at auction, although the buyer should have checked *AutoTrader* first as you can get one with 90,000 miles on the clock for less than five hundred quid.

6. A – The Met Office recorded the UK's highest ever temperature – 40.3°C – in Coningsby, Lincolnshire. Record highs were also set elsewhere in the UK, with 37.1°C in Wales, 34.8°C in Scotland and -12°C when standing next to Priti Patel.

7. **G** – The affidavit relating to the FBI's raid on Donald Trump's residence listed twenty-five documents marked TOP SECRET (as well as ninety-two marked SECRET and sixty-seven marked CONFIDENTIAL), although agents confirmed the former president had taken careful steps to redact them with a series of doodles and crudely-drawn moustaches.

8. **F** – Keir Starmer was found to have broken the MPs' code of conduct on eight occasions for failing to disclose interests and gifts on time, although some of them were Arsenal tickets, which understandably presents a dilemma.

9. **D** – England secured a 2–2 draw in the series against India, completing their biggest-ever run chase of 378, although normal service swiftly resumed as we lost the subsequent One Day International and T20 series in the weeks that followed.

10. **C** – According to the *Forbes* Tennis Rich List, Emma Raducanu made $21.1 million in 2022 (at its point of publication in August). Roger Federer topped the list with $90 million despite not having played a competitive match in fourteen months. Must have been doing a few car boots on the side.

THE NAME RINGS A BELL

They might not necessarily be household names, but the following people all made headlines in 2022. Can you remember why they were in the news?

1. Bongbong Marcos

    A. UFC fighter

    B. Nickelodeon presenter

    C. President of the Philippines

    D. Celebrity pastry chef

2. Chris Smalls

    A. Labour union president

    B. Canadian football player

    C. Lifestyle coach

    D. Scottish sports journalist

3. Maria Vorontsova

    A. Queen of Denmark

    B. Lithuanian Eurovision entrant

    C. Vladimir Putin's daughter

    D. Elon Musk's PR manager

4. Samuel Alito

    A. Prime Minister of Uganda
    B. US Supreme Court Justice
    C. French football agent
    D. Italian climate scientist

5. Peter Hebblethwaite

    A. Senior Met Police officer
    B. Australian oil magnate
    C. Shipping company CEO
    D. Cyber security expert

6. Caroline Watt

    A. Marathon runner
    B. Horse breeder
    C. PR agent
    D. Celebrity lawyer

7. James Cromwell

    A. American actor
    B. Descendent of Oliver Cromwell
    C. Evangelical priest
    D. Crypto billionaire

8. Kamila Valieva

    A. Foreign Minister
    B. News reader
    C. Civil rights lawyer
    D. Figure skater

9. Rosanna Currans

    A. MP for Surrey Heath
    B. Black Rod
    C. Mayor of Dartford
    D. *Songs of Praise* presenter

10. Halima Cissé

    A. Gymnast
    B. Mother of nonuplets
    C. Vaccine scientist
    D. Political journalist

THE NAME RINGS A BELL – ANSWERS

1. C – Bongbong Marcos (real name Ferdinand Romualdez Marcos Jr) won the 2022 Philippines election, after the majority of voters agreed it would be a laugh to have a president called Bongbong.

2. A – Chris Smalls leads the Amazon Labor Union, which in April forced the company to recognise a trade union in the US for the first time. Smalls further cemented his cult-hero status the following month after meeting Joe Biden at the White House while wearing a jacket with 'EAT THE RICH' emblazoned across the front and back.

3. C – Vorontsova is the eldest child of Vladimir Putin, who pulled the most embarrassing dad move possible in 2022 by killing thousands of innocent people and crippling multiple economies for a laugh.

4. B – There were widespread protests when a leaked opinion from the Supreme Court's Justice Alito showed that they were seeking to overturn Roe vs Wade – which they did in June – making women more regulated than guns in the process.

5. C – CEO of P&O Ferries Peter Hebblethwaite became one of 2022's leading villains after eight hundred of his staff were laid off over a Zoom call. You'll be happy to know he got his comeuppance in April when he was [checks notes] appointed to an additional cushy directorship within the company.

6. C – Rebekah Vardy's PR agent Caroline Watt found herself at the centre of her client's bitter 'Wagatha Christie' court case, and is perhaps best known for the unbelievable stroke of bad luck she had when her phone – and all the text messages within – accidentally fell into the North Sea.

7. A – Cromwell is perhaps best known for playing Logan Roy's brother Ewan in *Succession*, and is the tallest actor (6 ft 7 in) to be nominated for an Academy Award. In 2022 he made headlines when he superglued himself to a New York Starbucks counter to protest their policy of charging extra for plant-based milk.

8. D – Valieva – one of the world's top figure skaters – hit the headlines during the Winter Olympics in February after competing despite failing a doping test. Perhaps fortunately for Valieva, history books will probably skip over it when looking back at Russian news stories from 2022.

9. C – Conservative mayor of Dartford Rosanna Currans sparked outrage in May when she was photographed smiling while council leader Jeremy Kite cut a ribbon to celebrate the opening of a new food bank. People were right to be outraged – nothing says 'broken Britain' quite like wasting a perfectly good ribbon.

10. B – Halima Cissé is mother to the world's only nonuplets, who celebrated their first birthday this year. Doctors say the babies are in perfect health and, all being well, Cissé is on track to achieve a full night's sleep by 2032.

MAY THE LEAST WORST PERSON WIN

What's a more exciting prospect than a Conservative Party leadership contest? Well, lots of things – dropping a microwave on your foot, for example – but the race to succeed Boris Johnson had all the makings of a classic: treachery, deceit, some bloke you've never heard of ... Here are ten questions about Liz Truss's route to the top job.

1. Which ambitious backbencher decided to throw their hat into the ring, despite only having forty-eight hours of ministerial experience?

   A. James Grundy

   B. Nusrat Ghani

   C. Mark Jenkinson

   D. Rehman Chishti

2. Nadhim Zahawi decided to use NZ4PM as his leadership election tag, but the website NZ4PM.com redirected people to where?

   A. A porn site

   B. A video of a man fighting a bear

   C. A rival candidate's campaign website

   D. A fundraising page for Julian Assange

3. What setback did Liz Truss suffer following the launch of her leadership bid on 14 July?

    A. She got lost trying to exit the room

    B. Her microphone was still turned on

    C. A protester glued himself to the lectern

    D. She tripped while leaving the stage

4. As Rishi Sunak and Liz Truss were revealed as the final two candidates, more than ten thousand Conservative members wrote to party chairman Andrew Stephenson asking him to do what?

    A. Add Boris Johnson to the ballot

    B. Declare the contest null and void

    C. Call a general election

    D. Publicly support Liz Truss

5. As Rishi Sunak prepared to head out on the campaign trail, he presented journalists with a carefully focus-grouped 'Ready for Rishi' treat box containing a chocolate bar and a drink. What were they?

    A. Bounty and Dr Pepper

    B. Snickers and Coke

    C. Twix and Sprite

    D. Mars and Fanta

6. The Truss vs Sunak saga consisted of a seemingly endless stream of debates, but why did the TalkTV iteration on 26 July come to an abrupt end?

    A. There was a power cut

    B. Sunak stormed off the stage

    C. The host collapsed

    D. It was superseded by a bigger story

7. During an appearance on ITV on 18 August, Rishi Sunak said that one of his favourite things to order at McDonald's was the breakfast wrap. Why was this peculiar?

    A. He'd previously said he'd never eaten fast food

    B. He'd never been to McDonald's

    C. The item was no longer on the menu

    D. He's vegan

8. While the leadership contest was boring the UK to tears and the cost-of-living crisis worsened by the day, Boris Johnson holidayed in which two European countries?

    A. France and Cyprus

    B. Slovenia and Greece

    C. Croatia and Portugal

    D. Italy and Spain

9. Under normal circumstances outgoing and incoming prime ministers make the short trip to Buckingham Palace, but due to the Queen's mobility issues, it was revealed that Boris Johnson and his successor would have to travel to which other royal residence to complete the transition of power?

    A. Windsor Castle

    B. Highgrove House

    C. Sandringham House

    D. Balmoral Castle

10. Liz Truss's final TV appearance before being named PM was overshadowed by comedian Joe Lycett, who described himself as what?

    A. A champagne socialist

    B. Liz Truss's number one fan

    C. Incredibly right-wing

    D. An anarchist

May the Least Worst Person Win – Answers

1. D – Shockingly, Rehman Chishti didn't become Prime Minister, nor did he generate enough support to make it to the first round, or even find someone willing to back him. In fact, thinking about it, it's not 100 per cent certain that he's even a real person.

2. C – NZ4PM.com redirected to Penny Mordaunt's campaign website, which was using the slightly catchier 'PM4PM' as her election tag, so this leadership contest really did have it all, with the exception of vowels.

3. A – After her speech, a confused-looking Liz Truss sauntered vaguely towards the back of the room before aides showed her that exits are usually denoted by a big wooden rectangle that swings open when you push it.

4. A – They demanded that the ballot also included Boris Johnson as he 'got Brexit done'. If only there were a phrase about losing and subsequently getting over it that could be applied here . . .

5. C – The box that Rishi Sunak gave to journalists contained a Twix, a can of Sprite and a bottle of suntan lotion with the message 'Just a little something to make sure you protect yourself in this hot weather'. After all, how better to cool down on a hot day than with a refreshing Twix.

6. C – The debate ended when host Kate McCann fainted live on air, although it will mainly be remembered for the unprecedented three seconds of human emotion displayed by Liz Truss when it happened.

7. C – Sunak claimed that his favourite McDonald's order was the breakfast wrap, which was a tad surprising as it hadn't been on the menu for more than two-and-a-half years. He attempted to connect with the common man again the following day when he told a hustings audience in Manchester that he hoped his beloved Southampton would beat Man U that weekend, which would have been a tough ask since they were playing Leicester.

8. B – Boris Johnson went on holiday to Slovenia, returned to the UK for a few days, couldn't really find anything to do and jetted off to Greece.

9. D – It was Balmoral. Say what you will about the Queen, but making Boris Johnson travel all the way to Scotland just to pick up his P45 was an excellent prank, and pretending not to be in when he arrived was the cherry on the cake.

10. C – Joe Lycett caused havoc during the first episode of Laura Kuenssberg's new BBC show on 4 September simply by claiming Liz Truss was very clear in her answers and that he trusted her plans to address the many crises facing the UK. The following day's *Daily Mail* ran the headline 'NOW BBC COMIC MOCKS LIZ TRUSS' (the previous day's *Mail on Sunday* fumed about Boris Johnson being referred to as a 'cosmic cunt' on *Have I Got News for You*), marking a slight departure from their usual stance of blindly defending free speech at all costs.

ALL MIXED UP – ROUND 2

Some more anagrams to unscramble, because yhw otn?

1. JINK MUNGO – East Asian leader. Uncharacteristically wore an 80s-style leather jacket and sunglasses in March, instantly becoming a Twitter meme in the process.
2. BALLAST LECTURE – Well-regarded Netflix spin-off. Final season aired in 2022.
3. HARRODS MANIC – Novelist and TV presenter. Left popular quiz show in May.
4. SKEET SNOB – English cricketer. Received a promotion in April.
5. RIBBER SHEEPDOG – US singer. Supported The Rolling Stones at their BST Hyde Park shows over the summer.
6. ANY DRYDEN – British soap actor. Filmed scenes with royalty during the jubilee celebrations.
7. ANAL CRAZE LOVE – Professional boxer. Lost for only the second time in sixty-two professional fights in May.
8. PICKIER TEA – Former model. Admitted breaching restraining order in May.
9. BENCHER LEMONY – US comedy actor. Part owner of a British football club that finished second in the National League before losing in the play-offs.

10. CROSSWIND JUDI MONORAIL – 2022 summer blockbuster. Sixth film in franchise.

11. RAVE SCENE – Apple TV psychological thriller that debuted in February. Directed by Ben Stiller.

12. BARK LUNAR – New Zealand actor. Star of gory comic adaptation *The Boys*, which was renewed for a fourth season in June.

13. AIRSICK GYVER – British comedian. Caused a stir with his new Netflix special.

14. CHOMP DEEDEE – British electronic group. Lost their keyboardist in May.

15. DAHLIA NYLONS – US actress. The voice of Prime Video's 2022 reality show *Lovestruck High*.

16. BORN SLACKER – Former UFC fighter. Lost the WWE title at Wrestlemania 38 in April.

17. HANDYMAN RUB – Current British mayor who continued to poll well with Labour supporters in 2022. Surname means to overcook meat.

18. KILT SILVA THICKO – Also a mayor. Formerly a very successful sportsman but faced his biggest fight yet in 2022.

19. IDLING LAMP – Former *Hollyoaks* star. Can now be found travelling space and time.

20. GROWL JINK – Bestselling author. Spent some of the year discussing trans rights.

21. MINT SMEAR – German rock band. 2022 world tour stopped off in Cardiff and – for some reason – Coventry.

22. DANCE DINAR JAR – Foreign prime minister. Praised for Harvard gun control speech in May.

23. KING REHEAT – Football manager who signed with an English club in 2022. Likes to wear a suit.

24. KNEEL VIGIL – British drama. Wrapped up in April with a poorly received finale. Like a lot of expensive dramas, went on for too long with no idea of how to finish.

25. ACORNS IDEALIZE TOXOCARA – Left-leaning US politician. Announced her engagement in May.

All Mixed Up – Round 2 Answers

1. Kim Jong-un

2. *Better Call Saul*

3. Richard Osman

4. Ben Stokes

5. Phoebe Bridgers

6. Danny Dyer

7. Canelo Álvarez

8. Katie Price

9. Rob McElhenney

10. *Jurassic World Dominion*

11. *Severance*

12. Karl Urban

13. Ricky Gervais

14. Depeche Mode

15. Lindsay Lohan

16. Brock Lesnar

17. Andy Burnham

18. Vitali Klitschko

19. Mandip Gill

20. J.K. Rowling

21. Rammstein

22. Jacinda Ardern

23. Erik ten Hag

24. *Killing Eve*

25. Alexandria Ocasio-Cortez

THE EYES HAVE IT, THE EYES HAVE IT

The following people have all made headlines in 2022, but can you identify them from just their eyes?

1.

6.

2.

7.

3.

8.

4.

9.

5.

10.

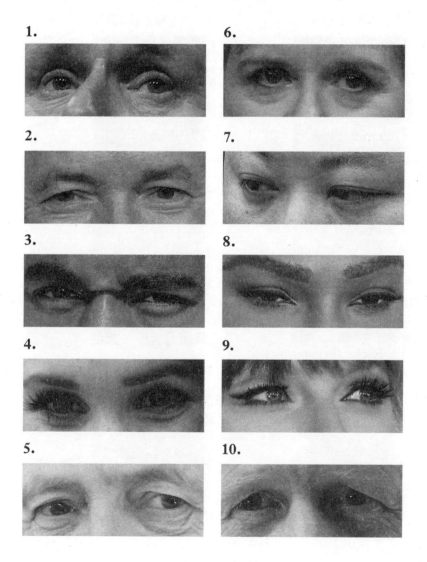

The Eyes Have It, The Eyes Have It – Answers

1. Keir Starmer

2. Piers Morgan

3. Kanye West

4. Meghan Markle

5. Jeremy Corbyn

6. Nicola Sturgeon

7. Kim Jong-un

9. Taylor Swift

8. Serena Williams

10. Boris Johnson

Tempers flared in Rome after an elderly driver was cut up by a BMW on the way to work:

IT'S A ROYAL COCK-UP – ROUND 2

Ten more questions about Britain's most famous family (after the Mitchells and the Slaters of course).

1. For reasons known only to themselves, Prince Edward and Sophie also headed out on a royal visit to the Caribbean in 2022. When they arrived in Saint Lucia a photo of Prime Minister Philip J. Pierre went viral after they presented him with what?

    A. A portrait of the Queen
    B. Commemorative stamps
    C. A photo of themselves
    D. Diamond-encrusted cufflinks

2. When a Chinese company attempted to cash in on the Queen's Platinum Jubilee, what glaring mistake did they discover on 10,800 plates, mugs and teacups when they came off the production line?

    A. They featured the wrong queen
    B. They said 'Diamond Jubilee'
    C. Jubilee was spelled 'jubbly'
    D. They said '700 years on the throne'

3. What did Spice Girl Mel B reveal after being
    appointed an MBE by Prince William at Buckingham
    Palace?

    A. She was bitten by a corgi
    B. She called him 'your honour'
    C. She burped
    D. She wasn't wearing underwear

4. As part of the jubilee celebrations, Fortnum and
    Mason launched a nationwide competition to find the
    perfect what?

    A. Pudding
    B. Cake
    C. Sandwich
    D. Summer cocktail

5. Which member of the royal family was booed by fans
    at the 2022 FA Cup final?

    A. King (then Prince) Charles
    B. Princess Anne
    C. Prince William
    D. Zara Tindall

6. The Queen made an unexpected public appearance in
    May at the opening of a new what?

    A. Statue of Margaret Thatcher
    B. Rail line
    C. Modern art gallery
    D. Post office in Chippenham

7. And speaking of unexpected appearances, Charles and Camilla showed up during an episode of which soap?

    A. *Coronation Street*

    B. *EastEnders*

    C. *The Archers*

    D. *Hollyoaks*

8. To commemorate his fortieth birthday, the Royal Mint released a special £5 Prince William coin, but what aspect of his portrait was not exactly true to life?

    A. His teeth were massive

    B. He was missing an ear

    C. He had hair

    D. He was slightly cross-eyed

9. One senior royal who was conspicuously absent from the Platinum Jubilee festivities was Prince Andrew. What reason was given for his last-minute no-show?

    A. He didn't want to be a distraction

    B. He missed his train to London

    C. He'd tested positive for Covid

    D. His sweat glands had kicked back in

10. Released to coincide with the jubilee, a song called 'Prince Andrew is a Sweaty Nonce' reached number 20 in the UK singles chart, by which band?

    A. The Tits
    B. The Twats
    C. The Arseholes
    D. The Kunts

It's a Royal Cock-up – Round 2 Answers

1. C – They gave the PM a framed photograph of themselves, despite the Saint Lucian version of Larry the Cat already having a perfectly serviceable litter tray.

2. C – Instead of Platinum Jubilee, every single item congratulated Her Majesty on celebrating her 'Platinum Jubbly', rendering them absolutely worthless outside of Peckham.

3. D – Scary Spice Mel B (now Scary Spice MBE) revealed that she wasn't wearing underwear beneath her dress on this occasion; or indeed any occasion – as she so very eloquently put it – 'I was stark bollock naked'.

4. A – The search for the perfect pudding culminated in May when a lemon trifle was named 'platinum pudding', joining Victoria sponge and coronation chicken on the list of food with royal ties, although the fact you've probably already forgotten about it doesn't bode well for its place in British history.

5. C – Prince William was booed as he was introduced at Wembley before the game between Liverpool and Chelsea in May. The *Daily Mail* ran a furious front page about it the following day, which must have been a misprint since they'd spent the previous decade harping on about free speech.

6. B – The Queen appeared at the opening of London's new Elizabeth Line, as she was one of the few people in the UK yet to be priced out of rail travel.

7. B – Charles and Camilla showed up in Albert Square to mark the Queen's Platinum Jubilee. Their performance was a bit on the wooden side, much to the relief of the regular cast.

8. C – The image of Prince William on the coin had significantly more hair than he does in real life (three of them, to
be precise).

9. C – Buckingham Palace confirmed that Prince Andrew
had tested positive, and that round-the-clock support was
being provided for the virus at this difficult time.

10. D – Despite the success of the song, The Kunts were a
surprise omission from the Party at the Palace concert.

RUNNING UP THE CHARTS

Having featured on season four of *Stranger Things*, Kate Bush's song 'Running Up That Hill' broke a few world records after it reached number one in 2022 – thirty-seven years after its original release. Here are ten questions about other songs that enjoyed a new lease of life after featuring in films and TV shows.

1. The song 'Handbags and Gladrags' has been covered by numerous artists, including Stereophonics and Rod Stewart, and served as the main theme for the UK version of *The Office*, but who originally performed it?

    A. Van Morrison

    B. Chris Farlowe

    C. Paul Anka

    D. Johnny Mathis

2. This American rock song from 1981 found new audiences with not one, but three TV shows: first in a 2005 episode of *Family Guy*; then in 2007 during the last episode of *The Sopranos;* and finally in the first episode of *Glee* in 2009.

    A. 'Crazy Crazy Nights' – Kiss

    B. 'More Than a Feeling' – Boston

    C. 'Mama, I'm Coming Home' – Ozzy Osbourne

    D. 'Don't Stop Believin'' – Journey

3. Queen's 'Bohemian Rhapsody' – originally released in 1975 – enjoyed chart success again in 1992 after being featured in which American comedy?

    A. *The Mighty Ducks*
    B. *Wayne's World*
    C. *Death Becomes Her*
    D. *A League of Their Own*

4. LA indie-rockers Phantom Planet scored their only major hit when their song 'California' – originally released in 2002 – was used as the theme song to which American teen drama?

    A. *The O.C.*
    B. *One Tree Hill*
    C. *Beverly Hills 90210*
    D. *Dawson's Creek*

5. Which band performed the theme tune for BBC crime drama *Peaky Blinders*, originally recorded in 1994?

    A. Manic Street Preachers
    B. Therapy?
    C. Shed Seven
    D. Nick Cave and the Bad Seeds

6. Although a modest hit upon its release in 1988, 'I'm Gonna Be (500 Miles)' by Scottish duo The Proclaimers enjoyed success in North America after featuring in which Johnny Depp film?

    A. *Donnie Brasco*

    B. *Fear and Loathing in Las Vegas*

    C. *Benny & Joon*

    D. *What's Eating Gilbert Grape*

7. The song 'Stuck in the Middle with You' is synonymous with Quentin Tarantino's 1992 violent crime drama *Reservoir Dogs*, but can you name the band who sang it nineteen years earlier?

    A. Stealers Wheel

    B. Teenage Fanclub

    C. Spear of Destiny

    D. Terrorvision

8. Tears for Fears reached number three in the UK with their 1982 song 'Mad World', but twenty-one years later a version by previously unknown singer Gary Jules reached number one after being included in the soundtrack for which film?

    A. *Mystic River*

    B. *Big Fish*

    C. *Lost in Translation*

    D. *Donnie Darko*

9. 'Eye of the Tiger' by Survivor is synonymous with the *Rocky* films, but which film in the series did the song feature in?

    A. *Rocky*

    B. *Rocky II*

    C. *Rocky III*

    D. *Rocky IV*

10. In 1982 Sting starred in the film adaptation of Dennis Potter's *Brimstone and Treacle*, and reached number sixteen in the UK after recording which song – originally performed in 1929 – for the soundtrack?

    A. 'You Know I Had the Strangest Dream'

    B. 'I Burn for You'

    C. 'Spread a Little Happiness'

    D. 'How Stupid Mr Bates'

Running Up the Charts – Answers

1. B – 'Handbags and Gladrags' – written by Manfred Mann's Mike d'Abo – was originally released by British singer Chris Farlowe in 1967. The version of the song used for *The Office* was arranged by 'Big George' Webley, who also composed the theme tune for a little-known panel show called *Have I Got News for You* way back in 1990.

2. D – 'Don't Stop Believin'' by Journey returned to the charts a number of times, peaking at number six, but the acapella version by the cast of *Glee* reached number two, and it was every bit as bad as it sounds.

3. B – 'Bohemian Rhapsody' was famously headbanged along to in *Wayne's World* in 1992, when being associated with a Mike Myers film was still a good thing.

4. A – The dreary 'California' by Phantom Planet was the theme tune for *The O.C.* It peaked at number eighty-three in the UK upon its original release, but reached number nine eighteen months later when the show became a surprise hit. Hollywood actor Jason Schwartzman used to be their drummer, which is the only remotely interesting thing about this track.

5. D – 'Red Right Hand' by Nick Cave and the Bad Seeds served as the theme song for *Peaky Blinders*, which – like *Killing Eve* – went out with a whimper in 2022 following a poorly received final season.

6. C – It was *Benny and Joon* that made 'I'm Gonna Be (500 Miles)' a hit in the US, and also in Canada, where it's called 'I'm Gonna Be (804.672 Kilometers)'.

7. A – 'Stuck in the Middle with You' was sung by Stealers Wheel, who are best known for singing the song 'Stuck in the Middle with You'.

8. D – *Donnie Darko* was a moderate success upon its release in 2001, but gained a cult following when it came out on DVD and in 2003 Gary Jules' rendition of 'Mad World' became the most depressing Christmas number one of all time, narrowly beating the equally ridiculous 'Christmas Time (Don't Let the Bells End)' by The Darkness.

9. C – 'Eye of the Tiger' became a global hit after appearing in 1982's *Rocky III*, although it very nearly didn't, as producers initially wanted to use 'Another One Bites the Dust' by Queen but couldn't secure the licensing rights.

10. C – It was 'Spread a Little Happiness', which re-entered the charts after fifty-three years. To put that into perspective, that's almost as long as it takes for Sting to have four orgasms.

THE METAVERSE: DO WE CARE?

Why be depressed in just one reality when you could be depressed in two? (If indeed 'reality' is an appropriate word to use when discussing Facebook.) In 2022 the Metaverse was touted as the VR-driven evolution of social media by global mega corporations, the world's leading tech gurus and, for some reason, Nick Clegg.

1. Facebook's Metaverse got off to a predictably brilliant start by having to almost immediately implement a 'personal boundary' in order to combat what?

    A. Muggings
    B. NFT scammers
    C. Kidnappings
    D. Groping

2. In March, which historical figure announced via their (living) family that they were posthumously joining the metaverse?

    A. Mother Teresa
    B. Nelson Mandela
    C. Pope John Paul II
    D. Florence Nightingale

3. March also saw the inaugural virtual version of which real-life event?

    A.   Fashion Week

    B.   The Met Gala

    C.   Women's History Month

    D.   The Grammys

4. Nick Clegg, a man with a Gavin Williamson-esque tendency for falling spectacularly upwards, received a huge promotion at Meta Platforms in 2022. What was his new title?

    A.   President of the Metaverse

    B.   Chief Metaverse Officer

    C.   President of Global Affairs

    D.   Executive Metaverse Overseer

5. Unsurprisingly, brands quickly began exploring ways to shove advertisements down users' virtual throats, but why was Heineken's first attempt at Metaverse marketing widely ridiculed?

    A.   A glitch made their avatar nude

    B.   They accidentally promoted a rival brand

    C.   It caused the Metaverse to crash

    D.   They launched a non-existent beer

6. Graphics in the Metaverse are up there with some of the very best that the PlayStation 1 had to offer, but what was noticeable about Facebook's Meta avatars when they were revealed?

    A. They only had four fingers
    B. They didn't have legs
    C. They had photorealistic genitals
    D. They didn't have mouths

7. Early in the year, what comically stupid thing did Snoop Dogg, HSBC and Samsung purchase within the Metaverse?

    A. Plots of land
    B. Virtual shares in Facebook
    C. Luxury yachts
    D. Virtual Beatles memorabilia

8. What feature – previously seen in *Doctor Who* – did Mark Zuckerberg claim the Metaverse will eventually have?

    A. Virtual vacations
    B. The ability to visit different time periods
    C. A universal speech translator
    D. Synthetic smells and tastes

9. In the same interview, Zuckerberg also claimed that the Metaverse would largely be controlled by what?

    A. A hive mind

    B. Artificial intelligence

    C. Nanobots

    D. A robot version of Nick Clegg

10. In an article in the *New York Post* on 8 January, so called 'futurists' even claimed that virtual reality headsets might one day replace what?

    A. Mobile phones

    B. Laptops

    C. Televisions

    D. Glasses

The Metaverse: Do We Care? – Answers

1. D – Unsurprisingly, as the number of users grew so did the virtual crime rates. Although with Dame Cressida Dick being recently unemployed they missed a trick by not launching the Meta-ropolitan Police.

2. B – Mandela's family announced a series of NFT collections, and the opportunity to purchase tokens for access to virtual galas in the Metaverse and real-life South African safaris. Everything was naturally very expensive – so much for a free Nelson Mandela.

3. A – The Metaverse's version of fashion week saw brands such as Estée Lauder, D&G and Tommy Hilfiger show off different low-resolution outfits on soulless avatars, which did, in fairness, look marginally happier than their real-life counterparts.

4. C – Clegg's new position was 'President of Global Affairs', which Matt Hancock is rumoured to have applied for after misunderstanding the title.

5. D – The company claimed the launch of Heineken Silver – which literally didn't exist – was a 'self-mocking joke', but backtracked after drinkers preferred the taste to their actual beer.

6. B – Legs were omitted due to the graphical constraints of realistically tracking them, because nothing says 'fun virtual escapism' like receiving a shareholder update from 50 per cent of Nick Clegg.

7. A – How real estate can exist in a world that isn't, well, real is a question for another day, but it's reassuring to know that if you can't afford an actual house, you can own a low-res, pixelated one that doesn't exist for about 90 per cent of the price.

8. C – Zuckerberg predicted seamless universal speech translation, allowing users to be scammed out of their life savings without the frustration of trying to decipher broken English first.

9. B – Meta recruited one of the world's leading experts as its 'head of AI', although if he was any good his job wouldn't need to exist.

10. A – The article claimed that virtual reality headsets could one day replace mobile phones. Taking bets now on the first person to be caught playing up front in the 1966 World Cup final while driving.

Is This a Genuine Fake Story?

Conspiracy theories have evolved in recent years from light-hearted conversations about the moon landings, Elvis being alive and the Kennedy assassination to more extreme subjects like flat Earth, chemtrails and Hillary Clinton being a satanist who eats babies. Can you separate the conspiracy theories we've made up from the 'real' ones that are still going strong in 2022?

1. The Large Hadron Collider at the European Council for Nuclear Research (CERN) is being used to open portals to hell.
2. The original Paul McCartney will return to be Donald Trump's running mate in the 2024 presidential election.
3. Portland International Airport is a front for the New World Order.
4. The moon isn't real and is hiding a secret planet that will destroy the Earth.
5. Disney created *Frozen* purely to manipulate search engine results.
6. King Charles is a werewolf.
7. Finland doesn't exist.
8. Keir Starmer doesn't have a soul.
9. Earth was sucked into a black hole in 2012 – we just haven't realised it yet.
10. Footballer Paul Scholes has two identical brothers and the three of them took it in turns playing for Manchester United.

Is This a Genuine Fake Story? – Answers

It's worth noting that 'real' in this context means it's an actual conspiracy theory, and not, well, real.

1. Real – According to this conspiracy theory, scientists at CERN dedicate their entire life to studying physics just to perform satanic rituals in a tunnel in Switzerland (*Wall Street Journal* – 4 April 2016).

2. Not real – Whereas many people believe Paul McCartney was swapped out decades ago for a doppelgänger, running with Donald Trump is a step too far, as it's actually JFK Jr who is set to give the vice-presidency a shot, despite the minor inconvenience of being dead.

3. Not real – Not even close; certain conspiracy theorists actually believe the world is being run by the New World Order, Illuminati and Freemasons from beneath Denver International Airport, which is over nine hundred miles away from Portland.

4. Real – Apparently the moon (and depending who you speak to, the sun) is merely a cover-up for the mysterious planet Nibiru, which was supposed to destroy the Earth in 2003, then 2012 and again in 2017. Perhaps it noticed we're doing a good job of wiping ourselves out and went home (*Express* – 4 December 2017).

5. Real – A popular theory proposes that 2013 mega-hit *Frozen* was created so that when people search for 'Walt Disney Frozen' it buries information about another famous conspiracy theory – that Walt Disney was cryogenically frozen until the technology exists to bring him back, although this one is easily debunked as most modern microwaves could have him defrosted in under thirty minutes (*New York Post* – 20 February 2019).

6. Not real – King Charles is not a werewolf. There are however, people who believe he's a vampire, due to reportedly being a descendent of Vlad the Impaler, plus his ears are similar to those of a bat.

7. Real – Incredibly, there are people who don't believe Finland is real, and think it was in fact fabricated by Japan and the Soviet Union to keep people away from a lucrative fishing spot. This one is widely contested, not least by people who live in Finland (Culture Trip – 19 April 2021).

8. Not real – Keir Starmer not having a soul is a fairly common misconception, as people often confuse 'soul' with 'personality'.

9. Real – Another one linked to CERN, which theorises that upon the discovery of the Higgs Boson particle in 2012 scientists accidentally created a black hole which destroyed the world. Good luck explaining that one to HR (Megaphone – 29 May 2020).

10. Not real – According to Man U fans, there's only one Paul Scholes, one Paul Scholes, ohhhh there's only one Paul Scholes.

At the launch of *America's Got Talent*, Madame Tussauds came to the rescue after Simon Cowell got stuck in traffic:

Missing Words – Round 5

1. Out of control _____ steals £300 worth of food from Tesco
   LADbible – 17 May

   A. Guide dog
   B. Six-year-old
   C. Seagull
   D. Traffic warden

2. 'I make thousands from racy gardening snaps – people pay me to _____'
   Mirror – 25 May

   A. Pot out my sunflowers
   B. Hose myself down
   C. Prune my bushes
   D. Sit on stinging nettles

3. Video of Disneyland employee _____ goes viral
   Indy100 – 5 June

   A. Ruining a marriage proposal
   B. Sleeping on the job
   C. Punching a child
   D. Urinating in the log flume

4. Cat owner spends £80 to find out what's wrong with pet – only to find _____
Mirror – 26 May

    A. It died three weeks ago

    B. She's sick of him

    C. It's a raccoon

    D. She's pregnant with nine kittens

5. Tesco on thin ice with furious shoppers over £3.50 _____

Manchester Evening News – 26 May

    A. 'Browsing charge'

    B. Paracetamol

    C. Charity scratch cards

    D. Jubilee decorations

6. Welsh local councillor William Gannon resigns after repeated allegations that _____ 'undermining' his ability to work
Sky News – 24 May

    A. He is not Welsh

    B. He is Banksy

    C. He is cursed

    D. He is a vampire

7. Massive   underwater   volcano   home   to '_____' erupts in depths of Pacific Ocean

Mirror – 25 May

    A.   Undiscovered viruses

    B.   Prehistoric creatures

    C.   Flesh-eating plankton

    D.   Mutant sharks

8. Japanese man spends £12,480 to look like _____

Independent – 27 May

    A.   Mr Bean

    B.   Ash Ketchum

    C.   A dog

    D.   Elvis Presley

9. Bermuda Triangle cruise offers all guests full refund _____

LADbible – 26 May

    A.   After missing it by over ninety miles

    B.   Due to 'ghostly sightings'

    C.   If ship disappears

    D.   After insensitive prank goes wrong

10. Man in relationship with his _____ says he's in 'love' – and they even have sex

    Mirror – 3 June

    A. Lawnmower

    B. Washing machine

    C. Shed

    D. Car

Missing Words – Round 5 Answers

1. C – 'Out of control **seagull** steals £300 worth of food from Tesco.' The cost-of-living crisis reduced the UK's seagull population to a life of crime in 2022 as fewer people can afford to visit the seaside and buy chips in prime swooping locations.

2. D – '"I make thousands from racy gardening snaps – people pay me to **sit on stinging nettles**."' An influencer named Ari revealed how punters pay her tens of thousands of pounds to do various gardening tasks in the nude. The news was especially unsettling to Alan Titchmarsh, who realised he could have retired at forty.

3. A – 'Video of Disneyland employee **ruining a marriage proposal** goes viral.' As a man got down on one knee to propose to his girlfriend on a raised platform in front of the castle at Disneyland Paris, a park employee ran over, snatched the ring from him and asked him to do it elsewhere. Disney apologised for how it was handled, as they didn't figure out how to monetise it in time.

4. B – 'Cat owner spends £80 to find out what's wrong with pet – only to find **she's sick of him**.' A twenty-five-year-old man from Salford Quays took his cat to the vet as it seemingly wanted nothing to do with him, before being delicately told that's just what happens when you own a cat.

5. D – 'Tesco on thin ice with furious shoppers over £3.50 **Jubilee decorations**.' Facebook's Extreme Couponing and Bargains page labelled Tesco's range of jubilee souvenirs 'tat' and 'a waste of money', unlike all the other jubilee merchandise, which comprised quality collectors' pieces that will only shoot up in value.

6. B – 'Welsh local councillor William Gannon resigns after repeated allegations that **he is Banksy** "undermining" his ability to work.' To be fair though, that's exactly what Banksy would say . . .

7. D – 'Massive underwater volcano home to **'mutant sharks'** erupts in depths of Pacific Ocean.' The volcano is home to two types of mutated hammerhead sharks, whose heads have evolved into an Allen key and a spirit level.

8. C – 'Japanese man spends £12,480 to look like **a dog**.' A man – identified only as Toko – paid a company to make him look exactly like a dog. It's not known how he rated the experience, however, as he was impounded almost immediately.

9. C – 'Bermuda Triangle cruise offers all guests full refund **if ship disappears**.' Not to be confused with P&O ferries, who make their staff spontaneously disappear.

10. D – 'Man in relationship with his **car** says he's in love – and they even have sex.' The thirty-seven-year-old man from Arkansas, US didn't go into the logistics of having sex with a car, but it's said to be exhausting.

THE MAIN EVENT: 2022 FESTIVAL HEADLINERS

One of the highlights of the year for music-lovers was the return of proper live shows (rather than those dodgy lockdown gigs where you paid £15 to watch someone singing in a wardrobe). Can you work out the following 2022 festival headliners from three of their songs?

1. Band on the Run, Twist and Shout, The Frog Song.
2. When the Sun Goes Down, Do I Wanna Know?, Mardy Bum.
3. Supermassive Black Hole, Knights of Cydonia, Plug in Baby.
4. Anaconda, Super Bass, Starships.
5. The Bartender and the Thief, Mr Writer, Dakota.
6. Everything I Wanted, Wish You Were Gay, Bad Guy.
7. Crazy Crazy Nights, Love Gun, Detroit Rock City.
8. Blame It on Me, Shotgun, Budapest.
9. Chocolate, A Change of Heart, She's American.
10. DARE, Feel Good Inc, Clint Eastwood.
11. All is Full of Love, Human Behaviour, It's Oh So Quiet.
12. Christians to the Lions, O Father O Satan O Sun!, Bartzabel.
13. New Kid in Town, Witchy Woman, Life in the Fast Lane.
14. Send my Love, Easy on Me, Set Fire to the Rain.
15. Fear of the Dark, The Number of the Beast, Run to the Hills.

The Main Event: 2022 Festival Headliners – Answers

1. Paul McCartney *(Glastonbury)*

2. Arctic Monkeys *(Reading)*

3. Muse *(Isle of Wight)*

4. Nicki Minaj *(Wireless)*

5. Stereophonics *(Y NOT?)*

6. Billie Eilish *(Glastonbury)*

7. Kiss *(Download)*

8. George Ezra *(Boardmasters)*

9. The 1975 *(Reading)*

10. Gorillaz *(All Points East)*

11. Björk *(Bluedot)*

12. Behemoth *(Bloodstock Open Air)*

13. Eagles *(BST Hyde Park)*

14. Adele *(BST Hyde Park)*

15. Iron Maiden *(Download)*

YOUR P45'S IN THE POST

Boris Johnson, Cressida Dick, Wayne Rooney and Eoin Morgan are just some of the high-profile people who left their jobs in 2022. Below are ten quotes from farewell speeches throughout history, but can you work out who said them?

1. 'It's been a tremendous privilege to serve this country as Prime Minister – wonderfully happy years – and I'm immensely grateful to the staff who supported me so well, and may I also say a word of thanks to all the people who sent so many letters, still arriving, and for all the flowers.'

    A. Theresa May

    B. David Lloyd George

    C. Harold Macmillan

    D. Margaret Thatcher

2. 'My retirement doesn't mean the end of my life with the club. I'll now be able to enjoy watching them, rather than suffer with them.'

    A. Alex Ferguson

    B. Kenny Dalglish

    C. Brian Clough

    D. Bobby Robson

3. 'And to those who have not felt able to give me your support, let me say I leave with no bitterness toward those who have opposed me, because all of us, in the final analysis, have been concerned with the good of the country, however our judgments might differ.'

    A. Silvio Berlusconi

    B. Neville Chamberlain

    C. Richard Nixon

    D. Winston Churchill

4. 'Dear Brothers, I thank you most sincerely for all the love and work with which you have supported me in my ministry and I ask pardon for all my defects.'

    A. Rowan Williams

    B. Pastor Brian Houston

    C. Jerry Falwell Jr

    D. Pope Benedict XVI

5. 'From my first, in a small music-hall in Dublin, to my last, in the huge arena in Belgrade, it has been nothing but laughter and fun.'

    A. Terry Wogan

    B. Louis Walsh

    C. Cliff Richard

    D. Enya

6. 'Keep inventing, and don't despair when at first the idea looks crazy. Remember to wander. Let curiosity be your compass. It remains day one.'

    A. Steve Jobs

    B. Jeff Bezos

    C. Warren Buffett

    D. Jack Dorsey

7. 'This is the greatest nation on Earth. It has been an honour to serve it. I give my thanks to you, the British people, for the times that I have succeeded, and my apologies to you for the times I have fallen short. Good luck.'

    A. John Major

    B. David Cameron

    C. Tony Blair

    D. James Callaghan

8. 'I'm quitting while I'm ahead. I'm undefeated, only the second man in history to retire undefeated heavyweight champion. I'm very, very happy and very content in my heart with what I've done, what I've achieved.'

    A. Evander Holyfield

    B. Tyson Fury

    C. Wladimir Klitschko

    D. Lennox Lewis

9. 'I understand the anger and frustration that people feel. To all of you who lost loved ones, who endured intolerable loneliness and who struggled with your businesses I am truly sorry and this afternoon I am offering my resignation to the Prime Minister.'

    A. Matt Hancock

    B. Professor Neil Ferguson

    C. Shaun Bailey

    D. Allegra Stratton

10. 'We must never forget that while Americans will always have our disagreements, we are a nation of incredible, decent, faithful, and peace-loving citizens who all want our country to thrive and flourish and be very, very successful and good. We are a truly magnificent nation.'

    A. Barack Obama

    B. Bill Clinton

    C. Donald Trump

    D. Ronald Reagan

Your P45's in the Post – Answers

1. D – Margaret Thatcher (28 November 1990) announcing her resignation after eleven years as PM. In May 2022 a statue of Thatcher was unveiled in her former constituency of Grantham, coming as exciting news to local pigeons.

2. A – Sir Alex Ferguson (12 May 2013) to Manchester United fans after his final game at Old Trafford (although his last match ever was a memorable 5–5 draw away at West Brom a week later). Fergie is famously into his fine wines (his face is certainly the colour of a vintage red) and the comment about looking forward to watching Manchester United in the years after he stepped down has definitely aged like one.

3. C – Richard Nixon (8 August 1974) resigning after the Watergate scandal, which by 2022 standards would result in about three column inches and a slap on the wrist.

4. D – Pope Benedict XVI (10 February 2013) packing in the day job because he was too old to really do it justice. The Vatican learned from this by appointing sprightly young successor Francis I, who was barely out of school at just seventy-six.

5. A – Terry Wogan (5 December 2008) after making the decision to step down from Eurovision. Graham Norton has made the role his own in the years that followed, but there was always something oddly soothing about a softly spoken Irishman critiquing Latvian folk songs about badger farming.

6. B – Jeff Bezos (2 February 2021) announcing to his employees that he was standing down as Amazon CEO. On his last day staff paid tribute in true Amazon fashion by haphazardly stuffing a carriage clock into a 16 ft box.

7. C – Tony Blair (10 May 2007) announcing his retirement to constituents in Sedgefield. He did offer a brief apology for the times he'd 'fallen short', which cleared up that whole 'devastating war over imaginary weapons' thing.

8. B – Tyson Fury (27 April 2022) reiterating on *Piers Morgan Uncensored* that his fight against Dillian Whyte was his last and that he was going out on top, although the same can't be said for Piers, whose viewing figures fell by 80 per cent in the week following the show's launch.

9. D – All four of these resigned over Covid breaches but this particular quote was from Allegra Stratton (8 December 2021) who handed in her notice for joking about partygate. She probably feels a bit stupid now, knowing she could have just denied knowing what a party is and hung around for another six months.

10. C – Donald Trump (19 January 2021) in his farewell address before handing over to the Biden administration. The speech was eloquent, thoughtful and well written, suggesting this was the first time he'd ever seen it.

2022 General Knowledge – Round 4

Did somebody say 'any more general knowledge questions?' No? Never mind ...

1. When LBC listeners were treated to a one-off show hosted by Matt Hancock in July, how did he respond when a caller referred to him as 'a totally useless Health Secretary'?

   A. He stormed out of the studio

   B. He laughed and agreed

   C. He muted the caller

   D. He asked them out to dinner

2. 2022 Wimbledon finalist Nick Kyrgios is never far from controversy, but what unforgivable crime did he commit after his fourth-round win over Brandon Nakashima?

   A. He threw a ball into the crowd

   B. He swore into a TV camera

   C. He used a branded towel

   D. He put on a red hat

3. When NASA engineer Smythe Mulikan appeared on the Conan O'Brien show, what did he claim astronauts were strictly forbidden from doing in space?

   A. Shaving
   B. Masturbating
   C. Making political statements
   D. Wearing branded clothing

4. During a Republican rally in Alaska, former president Donald Trump refused to say which word in front of his supporters?

   A. Abortion
   B. Vaccine
   C. Election
   D. Fauci

5. The discovery of 100-million-year-old fossils in the Sahara Desert led scientists to claim that it's 'plausible' which mythical creature could actually exist?

   A. The Loch Ness Monster
   B. Bigfoot
   C. El Chupacabra
   D. The Abominable Snowman

6. Which veteran Hollywood actor took to Twitter to call for Joe Biden's impeachment, claiming the president had 'wronged this nation's glory'?

    A. Tim Allen

    B. Steven Seagal

    C. Clint Eastwood

    D. Jon Voight

7. In July, Keir Starmer sacked his shadow transport minister Sam Tarry for doing what?

    A. Abstaining from a vote on strikes

    B. Suggesting Jeremy Corbyn be reinstated

    C. Joining a picket line

    D. Ignoring a hosepipe ban

8. After a huge crash at the start of the British Grand Prix at Silverstone, which driver was lucky to avoid injury after skidding off the track upside-down and flipping over a barrier?

    A. Yuki Tsunoda

    B. Fernando Alonso

    C. Zhou Guanyu

    D. Sebastian Vettel

9. In June, which purported Covid treatment, popular with anti-vaxxers, did researchers find had 'no clinical benefit' against the virus?

    A. Ivermectin

    B. Remdesivir

    C. Dexamethasone

    D. Lemsip and chicken soup

10. Over the summer, a specialist team was despatched to the Japanese city of Yamaguchi after a number of children and old people were viciously attacked by what?

    A. Bears

    B. Monkeys

    C. Stray dogs

    D. A leopard

2022 General Knowledge – Round 4 Answers

1. C – Matt Hancock didn't take the comment particularly well, motioning to producers to mute the caller, which they did. After the show listeners urged him to persevere with a career in radio, as it greatly reduces the chance of seeing him in a turtleneck.

2. D – Kyrgios had the audacity to change into a red hat and shoes, despite All England Club rules stating that only pure white may be worn. He made it all the way to the final against Novak Djokovic, which was bitterly frustrating for tennis fans as it wasn't possible for them both to lose.

3. B – He claimed that astronauts were forbidden from masturbating in space as droplets of 'fluid' could cause havoc in zero-gravity. That's the official line anyway – it's possible NASA is just trying to save money on socks.

4. B – Trump refused to say 'vaccine'. He found himself in a tricky position because he spent part of the speech boasting that he was responsible for the US's Covid response, but acknowledged his supporters don't tend to like 'that word' so he purposely wasn't going to say it. Still, there were signs of progress elsewhere, as he didn't suggest mainlining Toilet Duck.

5. A – It was the Loch Ness Monster. Scientists had previously disagreed on whether Nessie may have been some sort of plesiosaur as they require salt water, but the discovery – in what used to be a river in Morocco – showed that they could adapt to tolerate fresh water. How one ended up in

Scotland though is anyone's guess – possibly a wrong turn at Portugal.

6. D – Eighty-three-year-old Jon Voight tweeted a video accusing President Biden of 'taking down our morals, our true gift of the land of the free'. Biden responded by saying he's not entirely sure who he is but it's nice to see young people in America taking an interest in politics.

7. C – Sam Tarry joined a picket line with striking rail workers and was sacked by Keir Starmer for making up policy on the hoof, although since nobody could afford petrol and only a handful of trains operated in 2022 there was no real need for a shadow transport minister anyway.

8. C – It was Chinese driver Zhou Guanyu who crashed out at Silverstone. Broadcasters tastefully didn't show any footage until it was clear Guanyu was OK, whereupon they replayed the crash from every conceivable angle in super slow motion.

9. A – It was Ivermectin, which – among other things – is used to de-worm animals. Despite being championed by leading medical professionals such as Laurence Fox and Joe Rogan, researchers in Brazil concluded that it didn't improve patient outcomes. Then again, who among us can honestly say they've never eaten horse-deworming paste for no reason whatsoever?

10. B – The city of Yamaguchi found itself under siege from rampaging monkeys that were attacking people at will and trying to snatch babies. Expect a question on the subsequent film about this in next year's quiz, unless rabid monkeys take over the world, in which case we probably won't bother with a follow-up.

CLOSE, BUT NO CIGAR

Rishi Sunak – rather predictably – finished runner-up to Liz Truss in 2022, but how much can you remember about the second-placed candidates in these other (mostly) recent leadership contests?

1. In 2015 Jeremy Corbyn won a four-horse race to become Labour leader – amassing 59.5 per cent of the vote – but which promising young MP placed a distant second?

    A. Andy Burnham
    B. Yvette Cooper
    C. Liz Kendall
    D. Lisa Nandy

2. Theresa May won the race to succeed David Cameron on 11 July 2016 without the need for a vote, as her would-be opponent withdrew. Who was it?

    A. Michael Gove
    B. Liam Fox
    C. Andrea Leadsom
    D. Stephen Crabb

3. Tony Blair became leader of the opposition on 21 July 1994 following a vote triggered by the death of his predecessor, John Smith. Who was runner-up on this occasion?

    A. Margaret Beckett

    B. John Prescott

    C. Robin Cook

    D. Jack Straw

4. Which MP placed second to David Cameron in the 2005 Conservative Party leadership election?

    A. Kenneth Clarke

    B. George Osborne

    C. Theresa Villiers

    D. David Davis

5. At last, a chance for everyone to show their detailed knowledge of the Liberal Democrats. Who did Ed Davey beat in the contest to succeed Jo Swinson as leader following the 2019 general election?

    A. Tim Farron

    B. Layla Moran

    C. Wera Hobhouse

    D. Daisy Cooper

6. In one of the closest results in leadership election history, who did Ed Miliband beat by just 1.4 per cent to become Labour leader in 2010?

   A. Ed Balls
   B. Diane Abbott
   C. Andy Burnham
   D. David Miliband

7. More recently, the little-known Member of Parliament for Uxbridge and South Ruislip, Boris Johnson, became PM after comfortably beating which former minister?

   A. Amber Rudd
   B. Jeremy Hunt
   C. Rory Stewart
   D. Chris Grayling

8. Being less popular than Iain Duncan Smith is a difficult concept to grasp, but which MP was handily beaten when the 2001 Conservative Party leadership contest went to a members' vote?

   A. Michael Portillo
   B. Bernard Jenkin
   C. John Bercow
   D. Kenneth Clarke

9. Keir Starmer gave hope to people born without a personality in 2019 by becoming Labour leader. Which MP from the left of the party came second in one of the dullest leadership contests of all time?

    A. John McDonnell
    B. Richard Burgon
    C. Rebecca Long Bailey
    D. Claudia Webbe

10. In the 1975 Conservative Party leadership contest, Margaret Thatcher narrowly beat the incumbent Edward Heath, forcing another ballot. Thatcher comfortably won at the second attempt, but who was the runner-up?

    A. Edward Heath
    B. William Whitelaw
    C. Jim Prior
    D. Geoffrey Howe

CLOSE, BUT NO CIGAR – ANSWERS

1. A – Andy Burnham – then Member of Parliament for Leigh – placed second on 19 per cent (Yvette Cooper – 17 per cent, Liz Kendall – 4.5 per cent). As Corbyn's massive lead over his rivals became apparent, a group of Labour figures including Tony Blair and Alastair Campbell warned that it would render the party unelectable, in a rare case of those two being proven right.

2. C – Theresa May became prime minister after the withdrawal of Andrea Leadsom. May entered No. 10 on 13 July and spent two years travelling to Brussels and losing Brexit votes in the Commons before walking off into the sunset just like her predecessor, except without the whistling.

3. B – John Prescott came second in a three-way vote with Tony Blair and Margaret Beckett (Blair – 57 per cent, Prescott – 24.1 per cent, Beckett – 18.9 per cent). Thankfully he took the loss in his stride, as historically he hasn't reacted well to having egg on his face.

4. D – Despite his undeniable charisn'tma, David Davis was actually the favourite to succeed Michael Howard until David Cameron's famous 'no notes' speech at the 2005 Conservative Party Conference. David Davis still sits on the backbenches, whereas David Cameron wandered into a shed on 24 June 2016, never to be seen again.

5. B – Ed Davey beat Layla Moran to replace Jo Swinson as leader of the . . . sorry, can't be bothered to finish this one.

6. D – Ed Miliband beat his older brother David to become Labour leader following Gordon Brown's resignation. In the build-up to the 2015 general election David Cameron famously tweeted 'Britain faces a simple and inescapable choice – stability and strong Government with me, or chaos with Ed Miliband'. We dodged a bullet there, then.

7. B – Jeremy Hunt never really stood a chance, receiving just over half as many votes as his opponent (Johnson – 92,153, Hunt – 46,656). Johnson ran with the slogan 'BACK BORIS', which Tory MPs enthusiastically did for just shy of three years.

8. D – Iain Duncan Smith became leader of the opposition with 155,993 votes to Kenneth Clarke's 100,864. Interestingly, Duncan Smith only just scraped through the third round, receiving just one vote more from MPs than Michael Portillo, which would have had a huge impact on the future of politics and steam engine documentaries.

9. C – Rebecca Long Bailey came second to Keir Starmer. The result of the vote was 'scaled back' due to the developing Covid-19 pandemic, otherwise it might have attracted a crowd of at least six people.

10. B – If you said William Whitelaw, you know your stuff (and desperately need a hobby). Edward Heath had initially been expected to win and stay on as leader, but gradually lost the support of disgruntled backbenchers. That'd never happen nowadays ...

NA-TO, LET'S GO!

NATO found itself in the news this year after Finland and Sweden applied to join, which wasn't exactly celebrated by a certain Russian president. Can you name the thirty member nations* from the anagrams and clues below?

(* As of 1 January 2022)

1. LABIA NA – Joined 2009. Was proclaimed the first atheist state in the world in 1967.
2. EMU GLIB – Founding member. Brexit secretaries travelled here a lot.
3. AURAL BIG – Joined 2004. Its capital city dates back around seven thousand years.
4. DANA AC – Founding member. Ryan Gosling and Keanu Reeves were born here.
5. AI ACTOR – Joined 2009. The King's Landing scenes from *Game of Thrones* were filmed here.
6. CREEP CUB ZILCH – Joined 1999. Always seems to do surprisingly well at the World Cup.
7. KAREN MD – Founding member. Has the oldest national flag in the world.
8. AEON SIT – Joined 2004. This relatively small country has more than 2,000 islands.
9. AC NERF – Founding member. Had a tense presidential election in 2022.
10. GYM NEAR – Joined 1955. Bruce Willis was born here, also in 1955.

11. GEE REC – Joined in 1952. Home to eighteen UNESCO World Heritage Sites.

12. UGH YARN – Joined in 1999. Its capital has the most thermal springs in the world.

13. ALIEN CD – Founding member. More than 60 per cent of its residents live in the capital.

14. A YILT – Founding member. Was under a dictatorship from 1925 to 1945.

15. IT LAVA – Joined in 2004. Home to Europe's widest waterfall.

16. HAITI LUNA – Joined in 2004. The last European country to adopt Christianity.

17. BUXOM GRUEL – Founding member. Boasts the highest minimum wage in the EU.

18. EGO NON TERM – Joined in 2017. Home to the highest mausoleum in the world, coming in at a staggering 1,657 metres above sea level.

19. DARTH NELSEN – Founding member. Inventors of the world's first stock market.

20. CERTAIN MANHOOD – Joined in 2020. Birthplace of Mother Teresa.

21. WARN YO – Founding member. Home to the world's longest road tunnel (24.5 km).

22. LAP NOD – Joined in 1999. Its capital city had to be completely rebuilt after the Second World War.

23. ALP GROUT – Founding member. Most westerly country in mainland Europe.

24. MAIN OAR – Joined in 2004. Home to the world's tallest wooden church.

25. LAVA OIKS – Joined in 2004. Has a capital city that borders two other countries.

26. LOIN VASE – Joined in 2004. Central European nation that is shaped like a chicken.

27. A SNIP – Joined in 1982. Second largest country in the EU.

28. TYRE UK – Joined in 1952. Not particularly keen on Finland and Sweden joining.

29. DEMIGOD UNKNIT – Founding member. Was in the EU until very recently.

30. DENTIST SAUTE – Founding member. Found on the other side of the Atlantic.

NA-TO, LET'S GO! – ANSWERS

1. Albania	**16.** Lithuania
2. Belgium	**17.** Luxembourg
3. Bulgaria	**18.** Montenegro
4. Canada	**19.** Netherlands
5. Croatia	**20.** North Macedonia
6. Czech Republic	**21.** Norway
7. Denmark	**22.** Poland
8. Estonia	**23.** Portugal
9. France	**24.** Romania
10. Germany	**25.** Slovakia
11. Greece	**26.** Slovenia
12. Hungary	**27.** Spain
13. Iceland	**28.** Turkey
14. Italy	**29.** United Kingdom
15. Latvia	**30.** United States

HOW MUCH?????

Assuming you haven't thrown this book on the fire for warmth, here are ten questions about 2022's unprecedented cost-of-living crisis.

1. On 21 May Mail Online played down the crisis by revealing which household essential was actually 4 per cent cheaper than the year before?

    A. Shoe polish
    B. Pritt Stick
    C. Terry's Chocolate Orange
    D. Peat-free compost

2. In early June, the CGA hospitality industry tracker revealed the average price of what had reached £3.95 for the first time?

    A. A large portion of chips
    B. A pint of beer
    C. A small gin and tonic
    D. A pot of tea

3. After the Queen's speech set out the government's priorities in May, what did Conservative MP Lee Anderson say was to blame for food poverty during the subsequent debate?

    A. The war in Ukraine

    B. Brexit tariffs

    C. A lack of cooking skills

    D. The Labour Party

4. Everything else might have been mega expensive this year, but during the great two-day heatwave of 2022, UK cinema chain Showcase gave away free tickets to anyone who had what?

    A. Sunburn

    B. Red hair

    C. No hair

    D. No access to air con

5. While being grilled on *Good Morning Britain* by Susanna Reid about the cost of living – and specifically, the lengths that seventy-seven-year-old Elsie from London was having to go to just to keep warm – what did Boris Johnson incorrectly say he'd introduced?

    A. OAP energy subsidies

    B. Solar-powered 'heat hubs'

    C. Freedom bus passes

    D. Tax cuts on scarves

6. The devastating extent of the cost-of-living crisis was truly realised when McDonald's was forced to raise the price of what for the first time in fourteen years?

    A. Cheeseburger
    B. McFlurry
    C. Happy Meal
    D. Apple pie

7. As people struggled to afford basics like food and petrol, Ticketmaster came under fire for charging up to $5,000 for tickets for which US singer's 2023 world tour?

    A. Beyoncé
    B. Bob Dylan
    C. Lady Gaga
    D. Bruce Springsteen

8. As his leadership campaign faltered in July, Rishi Sunak began throwing out increasingly extreme policies to see if anything stuck, one of which was introducing a £10 fine for doing what?

    A. Dog fouling
    B. Missing GP appointments
    C. Dropping litter
    D. Mentioning his wife's tax affairs

9. In early July, photos on Twitter revealed that which dairy product was being sold for up to £9.35?

    A. Lurpak
    B. Mini Babybel
    C. Philadelphia
    D. Dairylea Triangles

10. And as if one dystopian dairy development wasn't enough, what did Tesco begin placing in tagged security cases?

    A. Yoghurt
    B. Ice cream
    C. Cheese
    D. Custard

How Much????? – Answers

1. C – Fortunately it's not all doom and gloom because we're paying 12p less for Terry's Chocolate Oranges, which – due to the circumstances – can now be classed as one of your five-a-day.

2. B – It was pints that hit the £3.95 mark (with some pubs in London reaching a frankly insulting £8) and nobody could afford petrol either, so with 99 per cent of the UK priced out of drink-driving at least the roads were safer.

3. C – MP Lee Anderson claimed food banks were largely unnecessary because a large part of food poverty was due to a lack of cooking skills, and that nutritious meals could be prepared for just 30p, earning him the unfortunate nickname '30p Lee' on Twitter.

4. B – The marketing stunt by Showcase offered free tickets to people with ginger hair, claiming they're more sensitive to the sun. A rather offensive move, although it might have boosted ticket sales if it didn't depend on ginger-haired people having mates to bring with them.

5. C – He was accused of being tone deaf after incorrectly claiming to have introduced Freedom bus passes in response to being told seventy-seven-year-old Elsie was having to ride the bus just to keep warm (he did expand the scheme so that it applied twenty-four hours a day on most services, but the Freedom Pass itself has been around since the 1980s). The appearance on *Good Morning Britain* was Boris Johnson's first since he famously hid in a fridge, which we'd strongly urge Elsie not to do.

6. A – McDonald's made the bombshell announcement that the price of a cheeseburger would rise from 99p to an unfathomable £1.19, which is especially devastating considering £50 worth of petrol will barely get you round the drive-thru.

7. D – Due to their 'dynamic pricing' system, which increases or decreases prices depending on demand, some tickets for Bruce Springsteen's world tour were listed at $5,000, which in the UK is equivalent to around three big shops.

8. B – Sunak proposed fining people £10 if they miss GP appointments, which was instantly discredited by economists as it requires getting a GP appointment in the first place.

9. A – It was the price of Lurpak that went through the roof. Bosses at Arla Foods, which owns the brand, said that prices were only going to rise further, and that the Lurpak Man – a symbol of wealth and decadence in the 80s and 90s – had been forced to downgrade from a trombone to a flute.

10. C – Images of cheese inside security tagged cases at Tesco went viral on social media over the summer. Perhaps Samuel Pepys was on to something . . .

Jacob Rees-Mogg's Benefits of Brexit Crossword

A mere six years after the referendum, No. 10 decided it was time to discover what we voted for and tasked Victorian London's favourite minister with finding out. Compiling all the benefits of Brexit into a single crossword was no easy task, so you may need to attempt this one over multiple sessions.

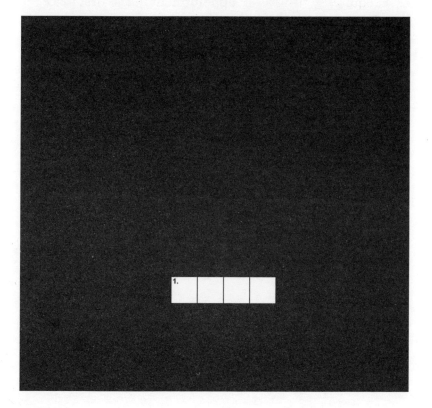

Across

1. UK passports are now this primary colour (4)

Jacob Rees-Mogg's Benefits of Brexit Crossword – Answers

Across

1. Blue

MISSING WORDS – ROUND 6

If there's one thing this year wasn't short of, it was absolutely ridiculous headlines. Have one last attempt at filling in the blanks.

1. *Love Island* villa surrounded by _____ as Islanders arrive for show launch
    Sun – 6 June

    A. Three-inch flesh-eating spiders
    B. 45mph attacking ostriches
    C. 40 million mosquitos
    D. Mysterious green fog

2. Putin's guards ' _____ on trips abroad to take home'
    Independent – 11 June

    A. Capture rare birds
    B. Take raunchy photographs
    C. Steal designer clothes
    D. Collect his excrement

3. Bizarre scenes as man seen _____ outside Hailsham Tesco

   Sussex Live – 13 July

   A. Walking a squirrel on a lead
   B. Riding a llama
   C. Punching owls
   D. Throwing sex toys at police

4. Man who 'feared his wife' refused to tell her he had a

   _____

   Indy100 – 16 July

   A. Water bottle stuck in his anus
   B. Vasectomy in an Asda carpark
   C. Thriving career as a gimp
   D. Insatiable clown fetish

5. Man left in 'burning pain' after mistakenly using _____ as loo roll

   Daily Record – 11 July

   A. Sandpaper
   B. Tesco toilet wipes
   C. Poison ivy
   D. Nettles

6. Mum astounded after finding giant _____ that's 'as big as her head'
Mirror – 13 July

    A. Cambodian oyster

    B. Hailstone

    C. Nine-inch fish finger

    D. Fossilised poo

7. Burger that tastes like ' _____ ' wins top prize
Pop Crush – 5 July

    A. Raw sewage

    B. Breast milk

    C. Dinosaur meat

    D. Human flesh

8. Chinese scientists invent laser so powerful it can _____
Independent – 22 July

    A. Reach the moon

    B. Slice through solid steel

    C. Melt diamonds

    D. Scar the air

9. Man wakes up after night on sleeper train to find
    _____

    Guardian – 22 July

    A. It never left Glasgow
    B. His clothes have been stolen
    C. Carriage full of pigeons
    D. His kidney had been removed

10. Footballer stretchered off after being hit by
    _____ thrown from crowd

    Daily Star – 20 July

    A. Chocolate penis
    B. Joint of ham
    C. Flying fish
    D. Live chicken

MISSING WORDS – ROUND 6 ANSWERS

1. B – '*Love Island* villa surrounded by **45mph attacking ostriches** as Islanders arrive for show launch.' Sadly, the ostriches were kept at bay, despite calls for producers to cover the contestants in bird seed and let nature take its course.

2. D – 'Putin's guards "**collect his excrement** on trips abroad to take home".' The practice is allegedly carried out to prevent foreign powers from gathering information about his health, although good luck explaining why you've got what appears to be nine Toblerones in your hand luggage.

3. A – 'Bizarre scenes as man seen **walking a squirrel on a lead** outside Hailsham Tesco.' Seems a bit cruel this – there's no justification for taking an animal to Hailsham.

4. A – 'Man who "feared his wife" refused to tell her he had a **water bottle stuck in his anus**.' This was in Iran. After the man's wife became concerned about his lack of appetite and apparent discomfort, he went to hospital to have the bottle removed. Some reports claim it was a Dr Pepper, although no proctologist was officially named.

5. B – 'Man left in "burning pain" after mistakenly using **Tesco toilet wipes** as loo roll.' A twenty-nine-year-old man from Wales accidentally used anti-bacterial wipes designed for cleaning the toilet itself, then did what anybody else would do in that situation: go to the press and reveal all rather than walk around like a penguin for a few days and forget it ever happened.

6. C – 'Mum astounded after finding giant **nine-inch fish finger** that's "as big as her head".' Amazingly, this wasn't twenty-five-year-old Shamima Trice's first encounter with a massive piece of food, as she'd previously bought a cabbage which was also bigger than her head, although it is possible that she's just got a really small head.

7. D – 'Burger that tastes like "**human flesh**" wins top prize.' A Swedish company called Oumph! created the 'human meat' flavoured burger. Good marketing ploy really, as anyone who claims it tastes nothing like human flesh will be immediately arrested.

8. D – 'Chinese scientists invent laser so powerful it can **scar the air**.' Researchers in Wuhan claim the laser can scorch images into the air that can be viewed from any angle and be physically touched, although it's feared teenagers have got hold of one after a crudely drawn penis appeared 3,000 ft over Beijing.

9. A – 'Man wakes up after night on sleeper train to find **it never left Glasgow**.' In fairness, the Caledonian Sleeper – one of only two overnight rail services still in operation in Britain – is operated by Serco, so it's no wonder it didn't work.

10. C – 'Footballer stretchered off after being hit by **flying fish** thrown from crowd.' Argentinian footballer Leandro Fernández was hit by the unusual projectile during a game in July. Sea creatures have no place in the modern game, and the upsetting scenes were condemned by a group of former players including John Scales, Steve Guppy and Prawn Wright-Phillips.

YOU WOULDN'T BELIEVE THE THINGS I'VE SEEN

Prior to her death on 8 September, Queen Elizabeth II had been on the throne for an astonishing seventy years. Can you place the following things that happened during her reign into chronological order?

Assassination of JFK

Cloning of Dolly the sheep

Cuban Missile Crisis

Inauguration of Barack Obama

11 September terror attacks

Live Aid

Chernobyl nuclear disaster

Demolition of the Berlin Wall

Suez Crisis

Death of Elvis Presley

You Wouldn't Believe the Things I've Seen – Answers

1. Suez Crisis *(1956)*

2. Cuban Missile Crisis *(1962)*

3. Assassination of JFK *(1963)*

4. Death of Elvis Presley *(1977)*

5. Live Aid *(1985)*

6. Chernobyl nuclear disaster *(1986)*

7. Demolition of the Berlin Wall *(1989)*

8. Cloning of Dolly the sheep *(1996)*

9. 11 September terror attacks *(2001)*

10. Inauguration of Barack Obama *(2009)*

On a Positive Note . . .

There's no denying that the majority of 2022 was exceptionally depressing, but if you looked hard enough (really, really hard, through the James Webb Telescope) there was the odd bit of cheer scattered around, so here are ten questions about some of the year's more light-hearted moments.

1. An undoubted highlight of the year was the news that Nazanin Zaghari-Ratcliffe had finally been released by Iran after the UK reportedly agreed to pay a decades-old £400 million debt, but what military equipment did the debt relate to?

    A.   120 fighter jets
    B.   5 warships
    C.   1,500 tanks
    D.   20,000 surface-to-air missiles

2. During a game against Brentford on 5 March, a clip of Norwich full-back Brandon Williams went viral after he:

    A.   Intercepted a streaker
    B.   Pulled off a perfect backflip
    C.   Hugged an opposition player
    D.   Smashed the scoreboard

3. In what could be a huge step forward in the quest for clean energy, scientists unveiled a computer that runs on what?

   A. Algae
   B. Fermented fruit
   C. Peanut butter
   D. Fertiliser

4. In May, firefighters in Yorkshire managed to rescue five sheep that had managed to get stuck on what?

   A. A canal boat
   B. The roof of a house
   C. The hard shoulder of the M62
   D. A light aircraft

5. In August, seventy-five-year-old George Miller from Scotland became the oldest person in history to do what?

   A. Walk from John o' Groats to Land's End
   B. Swim the English Channel
   C. Win a Commonwealth Games gold medal
   D. Graduate from Oxford University

6. Why did a chip shop on the outskirts of Coventry enjoy huge profits in 2022?

   A. It was endorsed by Justin Bieber
   B. It launched a Boris Johnson burger
   C. Bobby Davro moved into the flat above
   D. It went viral on TikTok

7. On 4 July, thirty-eight-year-old American Joey Chestnut won his fifteenth title in which competitive event?

    A. Thumb wrestling

    B. Lawnmower racing

    C. Hot dog eating

    D. Underwater tae kwon do

8. What was unusual when a single-engine Cessna 208 touched down in Florida on 10 May?

    A. Its propeller had fallen off

    B. It had run out of fuel at 12,000 ft

    C. A passenger landed the plane

    D. It was on fire

9. In January, the government fell hook, line and sinker for one of Joe Lycett's trademark pranks after the comedian tweeted a fake version of what?

    A. Rishi Sunak's expenses

    B. Nadine Dorries's phone number

    C. The Platinum Jubilee schedule

    D. The Sue Gray Report

10. During the season four finale of *Stranger Things*, an incredibly cheesy moment saw fan favourite Eddie Munson play which 80s metal anthem on his guitar to draw killer monsters away from his friends?

    A. 'Breaking the Law'

    B. 'Ace of Spades'

    C. 'Master of Puppets'

    D. 'Crazy Train'

ON A POSITIVE NOTE . . . – ANSWERS

1. C – The debt was the result of a cancelled order for 1,500 tanks following the Islamic revolution of 1979. Zaghari-Ratcliffe's release was on a knife-edge right until she boarded the plane, as negotiators desperately tried to prevent Boris Johnson from getting involved.

2. C – Brandon Williams went viral after hugging an opposition player. The player in question was Christian Eriksen, who hauled Williams to the ground towards the end of the first half, and although initially furious, when he realised it was Eriksen (making his first start since suffering a cardiac arrest) he warmly embraced him, much to the delight of onlooking fans. The sweet moment didn't last long, however, as Norwich lost 3–1, were booed off the pitch, and eventually relegated.

3. A – The computer ran for six months powered by algae, and was invented after scientists ran tests on a hundred laptops belonging to teenage boys.

4. B – Five sheep managed to leap onto the roof of a house in Newmillerdam from a nearby field. One onlooker said he saw them jumping onto the roof but nodded off after the first three.

5. C – Seventy-five-year-old George Miller became the oldest Commonwealth Games gold medallist in the B2/B3 mixed bowls. It just goes to show how training and nutrition has evolved the game in recent years, as back in the day many bowls players would retire at seventy-three.

6. D – For reasons known to absolutely nobody, Binley Mega Chippy went viral on TikTok in 2022, with hundreds of videos and even its own theme song paying tribute to the chip shop on Binley Road in . . . erm, Binley. In case you wanted to learn the unofficial Binley Mega Chippy theme song, the lyrics are: Binley Mega Chippy, Binley Mega Chippy, Binley Mega Chippeeeeey, Binley Mega Chippy.

7. C – Joey Chestnut won Nathan's Famous Fourth of July International Hot Dog Eating Contest for the fifteenth time after consuming sixty-three (including buns) in ten minutes, although the real challenge came later in the day when he had to get them round the U-bend.

8. C – Passenger Darren Harrison, thirty-nine, found himself in a nightmare scenario when the pilot of his plane became incapacitated mid-flight. With the help of air traffic controller Robert Morgan, Harrison (who had no flying experience) managed to land the plane and safely return home to his wife, who – as if this story didn't already have film adaptation written all over it – was pregnant at the time.

9. D – Joe Lycett tweeted a fake version of the Sue Gray report that accused MPs of singing Hear'Say's 'Pure and Simple' and playing a game called 'Pass the Arsehole'. It was clearly a joke, but sources inside Downing Street revealed staff were panicking over the 'leak' and in disbelief that Sue Gray would use the phrase 'down it street'.

10. C – It was Metallica's 1986 song 'Master of Puppets', which – like Kate Bush's 'Running Up That Hill' – enjoyed a resurgence thanks to its inclusion in *Stranger Things*, reaching number twenty-two on the Official Singles Chart thirty-six years after its initial release.

AND SO, TO 2023 . . .

So that was 2022, but how will next year pan out? Make your 2023 predictions below.

1. Will Liz Truss's government still be in power by next summer?

2. Is the UK heading for a recession?

3. Will Donald Trump go to prison?

4. How many cabinet positions will Sajid Javid resign from?

5. Will Labour announce a policy of some sort?

6. Can Manchester United finish in the top half of the table?

7. How long will it take for Ian Blackford to demand Liz Truss's resignation?

8. Will the cost-of-living crisis force the DFS sale to finally end?

9. How high will the energy cap go?

10. Can Ed Davey go twelve months without smashing a blue prop with a hammer?

And so, to 2023 . . .
Paul Merton and Ian Hislop's Answers

To tell you whether your predictions are right, we've consulted our resident fortune-tellers, Paul and Ian.

1. Will Liz Truss's government still be in power by next summer?

Ian: Is she still in power now? This book went to press five minutes ago. And anyway, is that a correct use of the word 'government'? I think it needs inverted commas around the word. As Health Secretary Thérèse Coffey has made clear, the most important issue facing Britain today is punctuation. She is concerned about Oxford commas, which means that we now have to put commas around any organisation led by someone who went to Oxford.

Paul: Who is Liz Truss?

2. Is the UK heading for a recession?

Paul: Yes. To make ends meet we will all become sex workers to visiting Americans.

Ian: No; I think that Britain's pork and cheese export markets will save us from the global downturn. The new 'government' will ensure that the UK will come to dominate the world economy with the Prime Minister announcing new trade deals with important countries like Legoland and possibly Poundland.

3. Will Donald Trump go to prison?

Ian: I am afraid that any conviction of Trump by a lower US court would be referred to the newly balanced Supreme Court which would then find Trump innocent until proved guilty. And then still innocent. Much as we would like to imagine the picture, I don't think we will ever see Trump in a jumpsuit that matches the colour of his face.

Paul: He is already imprisoned. In a prison of his own making. He is trapped inside the mental bars he has placed around his own mind.

4. How many cabinet positions will Sajid Javid resign from?

Paul: Forty-six.

Ian: Three. Or maybe five. Or maybe fifteen. Inflation is affecting everything.

5. Will Labour announce a policy of some sort?

Paul: No.

Ian: Yes. Of course. The policy will be NOT to announce any specific policies of any sort. It will be very definite about that and not at all vague. There may be shadow cabinet ministers who try and announce policies but this will not be tolerated by the leadership. Or maybe it will. That is absolutely clear.

6. Can Manchester United finish in the top half of the table?

Paul: Yes, top of the First Division.

Ian: Yes, I think that after some problems during the transfer window they have made a positive start and with a new manager, Erik ten Hag, who has made some changes to the playing style, this could be a good season for United and I personally would not rule out a place in the top four and a place in the Champions League, though again I have to say that both Man City and Spurs are looking strong at this stage.

7. How long will it take for Ian Blackford to demand Liz Truss's resignation?

Ian: I think he will do it within months, though Blackford will have to be quick to get in ahead of other opposition leaders who will be keen to make their mark in the new parliament. I am thinking of Boris Johson here. The ex-PM has pledged loyalty to the new PM and given his strong track record of keeping promises to blond women, a resignation demand must be imminent.

Paul: It's already happened three times but nobody's noticed.

8. Will the cost-of-living crisis force the DFS sale to finally end?

Ian: That is a very sloppy question including a split infinitive. As the Health Minister, Thérèse Coffey has made clear the urgent priority of this government is punctuation. It's all very well going on about the cost of living and how expensive sofas are but what really affects the wellbeing of the United Kingdom is the failure to correctly split an infinitive.

Paul: This is a very old joke, first made by Dan Leno (google him).

9. How high will the energy cap go?

Paul: To the top of the energy head.

Ian: The Liz Truss 'government' has promised that the energy cap will remain at a level that is somewhere between 'unaffordable' and 'eye-wateringly expensive'. The cap on bankers' bonuses will however not be capped and this will rise from 'a bit much' to 'it's the financial crash of 2008 all over again'.

10. Can Ed Davey go twelve months without smashing a blue prop with a hammer?

Paul: Yes, but only if he doesn't find out that his wife is having relations with a Smurf.

Ian: Who is Ed Davey?

BONUS QUESTION (WHICH IS IN NO WAY A PLOY TO PLUG NEXT YEAR'S BOOK)

1. One final question: how many words does this book contain?

Bonus Question – Answer

1. Find out in *Have I Got News for You: The Quiz of 2023* – pre-order now and see you then!

Picture Credits

27 Peter Rhys Williams/Shutterstock; 41 Maureen McLean/Shutterstock; 53 Chris duMond/Shutterstock; 69 Eddie Mulholland/WPA Pool/Shutterstock; 79 AnnaStills/Shutterstock; 86 A D. Ribeiro/Shutterstock, B Igor Bulgarin, C GEORGID/Shutterstock, D David Acosta Allely/Shutterstock; 87 A Nicku/Shutterstock, B Studio 2/Shutterstock, C Nadezda Murmakova/Shutterstock, D Stuart Bonar/Shutterstock; 89 Mikhail Klimentyev/AP/Shutterstock; 138 Kaca Skokanova/Shutterstock; 149/150 1 DFree/Shutterstock, 2 Kathy Hutchins/Shutterstock; 149/151 3 Mike Lawn/Shutterstock, 4 George Cracknell Wright/LNP/Shutterstock; 149/152 5 Shutterstock, 6 DFree/Shutterstock; 171 Stuart Wallace/Shutterstock; 178 Monika Hunackova/Shutterstock; 181 Robert Melen/Shutterstock; 205 1 Bill Robles/AP/Shutterstock, 2 Elizabeth Williams/AP/Shutterstock; 206 3 Elizabeth Williams/AP/Shutterstock, 4 Cheryl Cook/AP/Shutterstock; 207 5 & 6 Elizabeth Williams/AP/Shutterstock; 267–8 stas11/Shutterstock; 275 Graham Hunt/ProSports/Shutterstock; 289 Eric Johnson Photography/Shutterstock; 296 A Jimmie48 Photography/Shutterstock, B Featureflash Photo Agency/Shutterstock, C Frederic Legrand – COMEO/Shutterstock, D Rolf Klatt/Shutterstock; 297 Marechal Aurore/ABACA/Shutterstock, B Featureflash Photo Agency/Shutterstock, C Kathy Hutchins/Shutterstock, D Matt Baron/Shutterstock; 299 H K Content/London Entertainment/Shutterstock; 309 Jeff Gilbert/Shutterstock; 335/336 1 Rupert Rivett/Shutterstock, 2 DFree/Shutterstock, 3 Everett Collection/Shutterstock, 4 FiledIMAGE/Shutterstock, 5 LINGTREN.COM/Shutterstock, 6 Terry Murden/Shutterstock; 335/337 7 Alexander Khitrov/Shutterstock, 8 a katz/Shutterstock, 9 Kathy Hutchins/Shutterstock, 10 Michael Tubi/Shutterstock; 338 MAURIZIO BRAMBATTI/EPA-EFE/Shutterstock; 360 Image Press Agency/NurPhoto/Shutterstock